T0168551

Grounded

Forerunners: Ideas First

Short books of thought-in-process scholarship, where intense analysis, questioning, and speculation take the lead

FROM THE UNIVERSITY OF MINNESOTA PRESS

(Continued on page 72)

Grounded
Perpetual Flight . . . and Then
the Pandemic

Christopher Schaberg

University of Minnesota Press
MINNEAPOLIS
LONDON

An earlier version of "Sit Down, Be Humble" appeared in *The Atlantic,* December 1, 2019. An earlier version of "The 30,000-Foot View" appeared in *Real Life,* March 25, 2019. An earlier version of "The Flying-V" appeared in *Slate,* June 17, 2019. An earlier version of "Dwell Time" appeared in *Slate,* November 13, 2019. An earlier version of "Ode to Empty Airports" appeared in *Slate,* March 18, 2020. An earlier version of "Grounded" appeared in *Real Life,* April 20, 2020.

Copyright 2020 by Christopher Schaberg

All rights reserved. No part of this publication may be reproduced, stored in a retrieval system, or transmitted, in any form or by any means, electronic, mechanical, photocopying, recording, or otherwise, without the prior written permission of the publisher.

ISBN 978-1-5179-1202-4 (PB)
ISBN 978-1-4529-6591-8 (Ebook)
ISBN 978-1-4529-6613-7 (Manifold)

Published by the University of Minnesota Press, 2020
111 Third Avenue South, Suite 290
Minneapolis, MN 554012520
http://www.upress.umn.edu

Available as a Manifold edition at manifold.umn.edu

The University of Minnesota is an equal-opportunity educator and employer.

The airport seemed very new.

—EMILY ST. JOHN MANDEL, *Station Eleven*

The universe was not born to understand neologisms like *jet lag*.

—RANA DASGUPTA, *Tokyo Cancelled*

Contents

Preface

IN EARLY MAY 2020, I was summoned to have a recall service performed on my Subaru, so I reluctantly drove out to the dealership in Traverse City, Michigan, a half-hour away. I say "reluctantly" because I should have been sheltering in place, staying at home, staying safe—the novel coronavirus was spreading wildly at that point.

When I arrived, the service coordinator told me through her mask that the repair would take a couple hours. I didn't bring my computer to work on, and anyway they were discouraging people from lingering in the waiting lounge. But all the car dealerships are out by the airport, and I had different plan in mind.

While my car was getting fixed, I strolled about a mile over to the Cherry Capital Airport (TVC) to see what was happening there. A couple months before, before the lockdowns went into place, we had fled our home of New Orleans for the north woods, where I'm originally from, to ride out the pandemic spring there. Cherry Capital Airport is small but prosperous, its mere six gates belying just how busy a terminal it is. Flights into this little destination airport are usually expensive, and the planes are almost always full. On March 10, 2020, a press release announced that the airport registered a 67.6 percent increase in passengers passing through the terminal in February, compared to February 2019. At the top of the page, empha-sized in italics, this statement appeared: *"Growth Expected to Continue throughout 2020."*[1]

As I approached the terminal, I noticed a lone American Airlines regional jet on the tarmac—and it looked like it had been sitting there for a while. I had heard about all the empty airports by this time but hadn't experienced one directly. Being such a small airport, I didn't expect to be blown away, exactly. What made the empty terminals in the news so impressive was the juxta-position of the big spaces and no people. At a small airport, an empty terminal can just look like any typical day between flights.

But I was struck by the eerie emptiness of the place, when I walked through the sliding doors at curbside. No one was at the rental car counters; the check-in areas were dark; the security checkpoint was shuttered, and there wasn't a TSA agent in sight. The departures and arrivals board showed only two flights—and both were listed as *CANCELLED*.

I was the only one there; the scene was uncanny. Everything was ready to go, but no one was going anywhere. Standing there, I struggled to imagine this situation magnified to the scales of JFK or LAX or DFW—for all the interconnected logistics and networks making the fate of one airport a widely shared state of existence.

Suddenly someone came barreling through the sliding doors: it was a delivery guy, and he was grasping a tattered cardboard box. He looked frantically around and wondered aloud where everyone was—then asked if *I* could sign for a package. I sort of bumbled and said I hadn't seen anyone, that there didn't seem to be anyone around, but, I don't know, maybe I *could* sign

1. https://tvcairport.com/_pdf2020/TVC-Airport-record-growth -Febrary-2020.pdf.

for it? Luckily an airport worker emerged from the elevator at that moment and signed for the package—but he didn't seem happy to be doing it.

I kept on my excursion, wandering past dimly illumined check-in kiosks. Overhead announcements kept up their looped incantations: *Do not leave luggage unattended . . . Smoking is prohibited in the terminal building, except in designated areas.* The Business Center was desolate and cast in shadows. A pair of powerful pleasure boats sat on display, one near check-in and another in the baggage claim. They looked even more preposterous than usual, with no one milling about, no kids trying to climb aboard. A Hobie catamaran was also arranged near the front entrance of the terminal, with an advertising sign that almost taunted, "GET OUT THERE." I decided to leave—I'd seen enough. I walked the perimeter of the airfield, which took me eventually back to the Subaru service center. During those hours, I hadn't seen a single commercial plane take off or land.

This destination airport, usually a bustling little hub, had been rendered a ghost town—suddenly obsolete, abandoned like the aftermath of a sudden zombie apocalypse. And this was no anomaly. All over the country, and around the world, airports sat like relics, shells of themselves. People had stopped flying so abruptly that the silence in the sky could be deafening. What happened?

But first: How did I, a mere English professor, end up researching and writing about commercial aviation? I grew up as flight blossomed in the 1980s and '90s; I saw it die off and distort after 9/11, then regrow and metastasize over the next nineteen years. This was all after the so-called Golden Age of flight, in the wake of deregulation, and as air travel became a staple of professional and leisure life across the globe—at least for a portion of the human population who held class status or were upwardly mobile. It's important to remember than many people on the planet will still *never* board an airplane in their lives. Flying is not as ubiquitous as airline marketing paeans would have us believe.

My interest in air travel can be traced back to the years between April 2001 and August 2003, when I worked for SkyWest Airlines at the small airport outside Bozeman, Montana, then known as Gallatin Field. We operated three flights a day to Denver and back, on small, fifty-seat Canadair Regional Jets. That was the trend: smaller planes to connect more hubs and thereby connect regional airports around the country.

I was in graduate school at the time, studying American literature and environmental theory. I found myself paying attention to how the Bozeman airport occupied a strange middle zone in this place: It wasn't yet the great outdoors of the American West . . . but it was *almost* there, and made overtures to these rugged ideals through art, signage, and iconography.

During those years I worked the late and early shifts at the airport to supplement my small income as a college instructor. I found the juxtaposition of the mountains and tarmac activities endlessly captivating. There was something about seeing these lumbering planes loaded and unloaded against such sublime backdrops. Storms barreled through, and sunrises and sunsets cast everything in vivid hues—baggage carts and lodgepole pines could be rendered equally pink.

I was likewise enamored with the interior spaces, social codes, and design aesthetics that composed the terminal. Where are you when you're in an airport? Not really at your origin or destination, and not yet traveling. It's a lull, and sometimes an uncomfortable one during a longer journey. Airports are not meant to be stayed in, or not for too long. They can get annoying or claustrophobic really fast.

Actually, if I think back further into my childhood, perhaps my interest in airports began somewhere else, sparked by a gift on my seventh birthday, in 1985: a Lego airport set, #6392. This toy airport still delights me. My son Julien and I recently rebuilt it from our old pieces, using instructions we found on the internet.

In this compact yet three-story building, all of the airport activities and technologies are distilled: There is a check-in area, a waiting lounge, a restaurant, a clock for on-time departures, a control tower, and a checked baggage scanner. It's all there, in miniature and stripped-down form. And best of all, it's bright yellow! The audacity of that color choice is truly remarkable, for who would have thought to imagine the mundane airport as a bright yellow structure? (Well it *was* the '80s, I guess.) The exterior details of this set were also mesmerizing: from the runway lights to a windsock, from the baggage cart to a pair of marshaling wands. All these simulated details would later become real parts of my working life at the Bozeman airport, creating a small if meaningful experiential circle.

When I moved from Montana to California, in fall 2003, I began a PhD program at UC Davis, where I eventually wrote a dissertation on airports in American literature and culture. I went on to revise this project into a book called *The Textual Life of Airports: Reading the Culture of Flight.* The main point of this book was that the various stages of air travel involve layers upon layers of interpretation: getting checked in, navigating security (which got especially complicated after 9/11), finding your gate, knowing where to sit (and where not to), listening to overhead announcements, watching ambient TV (or tuning it out), and so on. While we think of airports as strictly functional places with clear directions for use, it turns out that all this reading and communication makes airports rife with ambiguity. (Full disclosure: a reviewer at *The New Yorker* called the author of that book "a touch insane."[2])

2. https://www.newyorker.com/magazine/2016/02/01/air-head.

I went on to write two more books about airports. In 2014 I wrote a book called *The End of Airports,* which recounts my time working at the Bozeman airport, describing what it was like to get to know the ins and outs of commercial flight—and then seeing it all change after 9/11. The second half of that book contemplates some more recent intersections between slick digital technologies (like smartphones) and the necessary analog clunkiness of air travel. By the "end" of airports I meant what airports had *become,* how they'd calcified into a familiar (if often contradictory) assemblage.

And a few years later I wrote a book called *Airportness,* which narrates a single day of flight and all the stages involved from wake-up to connecting to arriving home. In this book I experimented with a new form, really trying to plot out the time of flight as I took the reader through the day's journey. These books were all motivated by my teaching at Loyola University New Orleans, where I offered a seminar called "Interpreting Airports." This class became popular especially among international and exchange students, who had ample travel experience but were craving ways to think critically and imaginatively about these spaces and times. My students come from all sorts of disciplines, and I encourage them to use their own skillsets and perspectives to discuss how airports influence and affect the world around us.

Through all this writing and teaching, I became a sort of collector and anthologist of airport experiences, finding curiosities in everything from the subterranean baggage claim in my own home airport in New Orleans, to the glowing predawn gate areas of Stockholm's Arlanda airport, to the dazzling sound and light tunnel that runs beneath the Detroit's McNamara World Gateway.

I pay attention whenever airports are in the news—when they get disrupted, when they create space for interesting art, and when they result in unexpected events. I unconsciously track the flights each day as they pass over my Mid-City New Orleans, home, feeling the pulse of MSY eleven miles upriver. Without setting out to do this, I've ended up making airports a cornerstone of my career. And I've felt extremely lucky to be living in a town where a new airport was actively under construction; what a perfect research opportunity! My last book, *Searching for the Anthropocene,* ended with a series of reflections on this new terminal, as its final form came together and as the old airport faded into obsolescence. By the time I was finishing that book, I wasn't sure how or when the transition to the new airport would actually, in reality, take place.

By fall 2019 and even into early 2020, airlines and airports were reporting record numbers of travelers, with predictions that the swell would only increase in the years to come.[3] It was arguably new golden age of flight. Or, if not a golden age, exactly, perhaps a *plastic* age of flight: people were experiencing air travel as endlessly consumable and mass reproducible. But maybe also all too disposable.

Now it's late 2020, and commercial flight has changed dramatically, once again. The global pandemic caused airports to empty and most planes to stop flying—and those that flew took to the air with scant passengers aboard. People are slowly returning to the sky, but air travel is still down by roughly 80 percent as I finish this book. Many planes remain grounded in swaths along desert runways and will stay there—at least for the time being.

3. https://www.ajc.com/travel/airports-near-new
-passenger-record-demand-for-air-travel-continues-grow
/1sgMGmwN0pOvfHXdCrPE3L/ and https://www.cnbc.com/2019
/05/21/us-airlines-set-to-carry-a-record-number-of-passengers-this
-summer.html.

Sit Down, Be Humble

Why Cell Reception Is So Bad Right after Boarding the Plane

Our shared anxieties about flight were very different, not so long ago.

It's September 2019. I had just settled into seat 2D, and my seatmate and I were swiping away at our phones frantically. The signal was so sluggish that Twitter feeds wouldn't load, and email struggled to come through. Bars of service blinked between one bar and nothing.

Cellular reception is uniformly awful on airliners parked at the gate. But why? My own answers were hypothetical and vaguely conspiratorial: Maybe interference from the wiring or circuitry in the aircraft fuselage plays a part. Or perhaps a magic box in the cockpit somehow interrupts service to dissuade in-flight use. I wondered if a governing body like the Federal Aviation Administration might require airports to dampen the cell signals, or if some carriers were impacted more than others.

After that flight I asked three commercial pilots (two from Delta, one from British Airways), and they all corroborated my hunch that cell reception is particularly bad at this odd juncture pre- and postflight—for pilots as well as for passengers.

"There are certain areas of ramps and jetways where our ACARS uplinks are sketchy for the same reason," one of them, Mark Werkema, said. ACARS stands for aircraft communications addressing and reporting system; airplanes use it to communicate with one another and with control towers. It would seem like a safety concern, too, if bad coverage affects important communications sent or received by the crew.

Jon Brittingham, a technical pilot on the Airbus A319/320/321 program, explained the causes to me in greater detail. Older aircraft, like the McDonnel Douglas MD-90, don't have the same electronic-systems shielding to protect cabin equipment from third-party signals that more modern airliners, like the current Airbuses, have. In fact, this shielding is most dense around the cabin—thus confirming my pilot contacts' shared agreement about poor reception within the cockpit. (This same fact can also cause cell reception in first class seats to be the worst in the plane, when parked at the gate.)

Airports are giant swaths of empty space, where large vehicles exit and enter the sky. That makes them poor candidates for cellular-antenna towers. Towers might grace the airport's edges, but the expanse of airfields, and the distance to the terminal, makes coverage a stretch. To make up for it, airports use distributed antennae systems (DAS): small, targeted cellular access points (some barely bigger than smoke detectors) that work particularly well in indoor, controlled spaces. A DAS provider explains the particular challenge of airports this way: "These spaces are often challenging topologies that have high ceilings, wide-open areas, or are located in harsh environments that present a challenge to designing and deploying reliable wireless service."[1] *Harsh environments*—what a nice euphemism for the sound and fury of terminals.

---

1. https://adrftech.com/industry/transportation/.

It works, indoors at least. The Denver International Airport, for instance, has been lauded for its use of DAS networks to provide superior service to passengers in the terminal and throughout the concourses—even better than customers are used to at home in the suburbs.[2] But once you're sitting on the plane, the signal problems begin. As *Wired* reported several years ago, it may have to do with conflicting signals caused by the plethora of the small cellular antennae inside the terminal and the cell towers beyond the airfield.[3] (There's also onboard Wi-Fi, further complicating things. That's another issue, but one more reason why, as an old Delta ad put it, we've come to "expect the internet" when flying.[4])

Basically, on the plane your phone can't decide which antenna to connect to, and this confusion contributes to the slow service. It doesn't help that on any given plane, anywhere from fifty to three hundred passengers might be clambering for a signal as soon as they are seated or when the plane touches down. Pair this with certain aircraft models, like the Boeing 787, whose structural materials may impede cell signals, and you get a perfect storm of poor service.[5]

A coverage rift erupts deepest between the terminal's interiors and the surrounding cellular landscape. On the airplane, you're neither inside the airport nor clearly outside it—you're in a bizarre netherworld, where cell signals are muddled.

Bad service on parked planes becomes a useful parable for thinking about the overlapping promises of mobile technology

2. https://www.denverpost.com/2017/11/21/denver-international
-airport-best-cellular-service/.

3. https://www.wired.com/2014/07/airport-wireless/.

4. http://airplanereading.org/story/222/expect-the-internet.

5. https://fromhomeandback.boardingarea.com/2015/05/07/one
-critical-thing-i-learned-on-the-american-787-dreamliner-flight/.

and of commercial flight. I want to think that I'm at the center of the travel experience: it's my journey, my life, my social media posts. But complex infrastructure and collective behaviors make the whole enterprise chug along. In order to provide maximum service to users, the carriers oversupply the airport concourses, but at the expense of the expansive tarmac areas that fall just out of reception zone for the terminal antennae, which are also just a bit too far from nearby cell towers. It's a compromise carried out in order to sustain a larger (if always imperfect) arrangement.

When cell signals go dark on the plane after boarding, it's a low-grade reminder of how air travel is always woven into people's lives on the ground. Landing passengers need to communicate with family, friends, or drivers arriving for pick-up; urgent work tasks may need attending to, and an ongoing "searching" icon can be infuriating. It seems like these are two separate realms and they should connect more discretely, yet also seamlessly. But the truth is, flight is always messily entangled with infrastructural tendrils.

That's an anxiety that pervades airports, places where connections of all kinds get made and broken. There's a reason why the China Philharmonic Orchestra staged a flash performance at Beijing Capital International Airport in February 2019: It was sure to be captured by phone and shared online, thanks to saturated DAS antennae.[6] The autumn 2019 Hong Kong airport protests were effective because they interrupted the traffic (and thus economic) flows around the huge site—but just as much because these interruptions were disseminated via smartphones.[7] When Newark airport was suddenly and terrifyingly evacuated in September 2019, the chaotic scene was uncanny not just for

6. https://www.youtube.com/watch?v=ZQRKilvN_z0.
7. https://www.nytimes.com/2019/08/09/world/asia/hong-kong -airport-protest.html.

what it was (or wasn't) but for how it quickly dominated social media feeds far beyond the New York region.[8] Live shooters and terrorists preoccupy Americans' minds, and the airport was ready-made for an incident of this type. Airport happenings are primed to spread online.

Everyone is on edge at the airport. Will I make my flight? Am I a bad parent for traveling to make a living? Can I afford this vacation? Do I need this expensive bottled water, this crummy sandwich? Where's my ID? These agglomerated worries make it even more irritating when something seemingly simple, like mobile coverage, breaks down. But maybe the uncertainty causes most of the anxiety. Flyers are stressed about what they cannot control. In the face of ignorance, any knowledge is a comfort: You're definitely going to miss your connection, or, your bag is confirmed loaded on the plane.

When the specter of bad coverage takes your pre- or postflight calls and app updates out of commission, take it as another new certainty. There's nothing you can do but wait. It's not about you anymore, but an accident of infrastructure. Flyers might take this moment as a chance to feel humility rather than self-centered frustration. Look around, appreciate the complexity of the system at work. Appreciate that it works as well as it does, most of the time. Instead of searching for a cell signal (or an email, or an Instagram update), look for a signal of a different kind. Everything's going to be okay—and, for now, there's nothing you can do about it anyway.

The philosopher Jacques Derrida had a theory about structures.[9] For any given structure to work, it has to have wiggle room—

8. https://www.nytimes.com/2019/09/02/nyregion/newark-airport-evacuation.html.

9. http://www2.csudh.edu/ccauthen/576f13/DrrdaSSP.pdf.

room for *free play,* where the pieces that compose the structure can slip a little. Think of how buildings are built to withstand earthquakes, or how a steering wheel has just that wee bit of give each way as you hold it in your hands while driving. Or how concrete bridges use metal expansion joints to adjust to changes in air temperature. Cell signals at the gate are another example of this principle, where a system attempting to maximize connectivity needs some disruption, as well.

And no system is totally enclosed. There's always something extra, a remainder, which falls outside of or lingers beyond the structure. That's part of the play. Reception will be fine in the airport, or out on the road—it's just in a temporary abyss, right here. And it's not simply because you're inside the plane or outside the airport. It's because *inside* and *outside* are never neat and tidy distinctions. No wall can perfectly separate two countries.[10] The Amazon rainforest isn't definitively bound by its supposed geographic borders.[11] Residential air conditioners don't just regulate temperature indoors, but also send emissions into the atmosphere.[12] And airplanes on the tarmac and mobile devices in our palms are not only working within their own respective systems but are entangled with each other—and everything else.

Commercial air travel and mobile communications, awkwardly coexisting at the moment before or just after a flight, become an example through which we might better understand human beings as a *superorganism,* or a species whose combined activities over time form intricate patterns that span far beyond any one

10. https://www.theatlantic.com/ideas/archive/2019/02/trump -will-never-get-his-border-wall/582085/.

11. https://www.theatlantic.com/science/archive/2019/08/amazon -fires-are-political/596776/.

12. https://www.wired.com/story/what-if-air-conditioners-could -help-save-the-planet/.

single member of the group. Like ant colonies or coral reefs: millions of smaller units that cumulatively create something vaster and utterly indistinguishable from the individuals.

Picture flight route maps or cell coverage charts: crisscrossing lines, networks and grids. Such diagrams show that what humans are part of is never simply local, nor just abstractly global. Each connection made or missed, each signal attained or dropped, is part of a much larger structure—and the necessary free play involved therein. For it all to work, there are going to be places where it fails, where slippage can occur. This is terrifying to think of with respect to flight; less so, if more aggravating, to think about in relation to cell service. Together, though, they illuminate this massive process and the complex systems we're all a part of.

The Hong Kong airport protesters were described as a *swarm*.[13] The Newark airport evacuation exposed the hive structure of the terminal and how easily it can be upset—like poking a wasp's nest. When cell signals go dark on the plane after boarding, it's a low-grade reminder of how air travel is a superorganism phenomenon.

In light of all this, passengers might be more patient with bad service at the gate. Flyers might take this frustrating moment as a chance to feel humility rather than self-centered annoyance. There might be better things to do in this moment after sitting down on the plane. Look around, appreciate the complexity of the system at work. Appreciate that it functions as well as it does, most of the time. Appreciate all the free play that makes the structure work. Appreciate being part of a superorganism swarming around the globe, searching for signals. After all, it could be worse. Flight could become even trickier and less frequent. Cellular disruptions could come in other forms, forms far more grave.

13. https://fortune.com/2019/08/12/hong-kong-airport-flights
-canceled-protest/.

Flyover

Touring a New Airport on the Eve of Its Grand Opening

On Saturday October 26th, 2019, I went to an open house for the brand-new Louis Armstrong International Airport in Kenner, Louisiana (MSY). The airport was planning on thousands of people passing through the new terminal that day; originally the terminal was supposed to open at 10:00 a.m., but stormy weather had pushed the event back to 1:00 p.m.

The new terminal, set to open in two weeks, had a big PR problem: The airport planned to open before a dedicated fly-over ramp from the highway had been constructed. Everyone in town seemed to know about this, and most were grumpy about it. When I told my friend Tom that I was going out to the new terminal to write something about it, he remarked, "The flyover is the whole story." I was about to find out why.

I sped along I-10 highway past the old airport exit and then, as instructed, took the exit for Loyola Avenue. It was supposed to be three fairly straightforward stoplights, after which the new airport access road would magically appear.

I was immediately gridlocked in a long line of vehicles backed up at the initial intersection. Could this many people be coming to tour the new airport? But no, this was something else: the stoplight was out completely. In fact, as I looked around, I realized that all the stoplights in the vicinity were dark, leaving thousands of cars on four- and six-lane roads—with complicated double left-turn lanes—to awkwardly improvise four-way stops, for hours.

Post–Tropical Storm Olga had turned into a cyclone the night before, resulting in 60-mph winds that took down powerlines across the New Orleans metro area, leaving some places like Kenner without electricity well into the day.

At the third intersection on Aberdeen, a road crew was patching over a large section of asphalt, requiring one final detour. Then Aberdeen transformed abruptly into a freakishly new, futuristic-feeling approach road with roundabouts and manicured palms ... and suddenly the new airport appeared. Or rather, two colossal unmatched parking garages dominated the field of vision. The modern new terminal withdrew into the background.

I followed a series of understated EVENT signs around the roundabouts and toward the short-term parking garage. My nine-year-old son, Julien, who had come along with me for the tour, took pictures with my phone of the hulking structures as we passed them. We parked on the fourth floor of the garage, as instructed, and walked to the pedestrian bridge connector. As we crossed over, it reminded me uncannily of the short pedestrian bridge that connects the nearby Target to its own parking garage; I had walked these steps, before.

Passing through sliding doors we found ourselves in a small, nondescript antechamber.

"It smells in here," noted Julien. And then we were there: In the new terminal.

It was nice! It was bright, and the check-in counters swooped around in a crescent shape, presenting American, Southwest, Delta . . . and all the other airline logos receding around the bend. The check-in area looked surprisingly modest—it was hard to imagine thousands of anxious travelers milling about this space, dragging roller bags. The odd thing about this new airport being championed as a catalyst for growth is that it is, in fact, rather small.

We were given a "self tour guide" brochure, and a separate piece of cardstock paper with instructions for how to get back to the highway. (More on this, later.) We checked in with a volunteer who scanned the QR code we've been given when we registered for the tour, and then we were let loose. There were already hundreds of visitors disseminating through the terminal by the time we checked in, and we were among the early arrivals.

Other than the cyclone of that morning, it was a beautiful fall day, billowing low cumulus clouds racing across the sky, romantically framed by the new terminal's windows and skylights. There was something incredibly peculiar and delightful about this, milling around the new, almost airport with so many other residents of the city, no one planning to go anywhere other than *here*. People walked around with selfie sticks, or holding their phones out at arm's length while taking long videos as they walked through the terminal. It was the utopic vision of an airport, in a way: we had all arrived in this not-yet nonplace to simply appreciate its features.

But most of the features were still emergent, paused midconstruction. The computer screens behind the American Airlines check-in counters were shrouded with white plastic garbage bags. Delta's self-check-in kiosks looked barely put together, orange safety cones still positioned around them.

I stood soaking in the aura of departure and thinking about my faltered arrival by car. The infamous, absent flyover hung over this space like a concrete specter. Would this highway glitch doom the airport to come? Or would something else—a hurricane? a pandemic?

Descending the main bank of escalators, and seeing other escalators running aslant a floor below, gave the impression of an

M. C. Escher drawing or like a scene from the movie *Inception*: vaguely vertiginous, but aesthetically amusing as well. One escalator was already out of order—or perhaps it just wasn't working, yet. On the way down Julien remarked, "It's nice, but not as nice as our old airport. . . ." I'm pretty sure some people around us heard him; what a statement, especially when uttered by the youth. I couldn't say I disagreed, exactly. This terminal presented itself as a new airport, but not a significantly improved one. It's just . . . *new*. And it still seemed far from finished.

The piecemeal nature of the terminal was especially evident when we got to the security checkpoint, with its impressively open (if intimidatingly serpentine) holding area ready for the stampede of passengers to come. We all bypassed the security lines and filed through a half-constructed checkpoint corridor, with no fanfare. Pausing here, I noted that a majority of the checkpoints were only partially put together. Magnetometers and full-body scanners lay in fragments on the floor; computer monitors were still in half-open boxes, cords dangling out. It was here that I thought, *There is no way this terminal is opening in two weeks*.

In the postsecurity zone of the airport, Julien and I paused to consider our options. We could visit the A, B, and C concourses, and see the bounty that awaited future travelers. Mostly this meant the gate areas, storefronts, and eateries—themselves all in various stages of incompletion. We headed left toward the C concourse, first.

I'm sure a lot of planning and coordination went into the two public open houses, of which this day was the second. But as Julien and I ambled toward Concourse C, we couldn't ignore the general state of disarray. It was as if the workers had dropped whatever they were doing that morning and vacated the place without tidying up.

Doors were boarded up and taped over. The Delta SkyClub took the cake, with gaudy pink insulation sheet boards leaned against the frosted glass, barring entry, for now, to even Diamond Medallion members. Some walls were primed but unfinished; strips of blue painter's tape could be seen here and there; large information display screens were uncovered, electronics exposed. A paper towel roll stood in the corner of one half-finished shop. A five-gallon bucket lay upside down on a square of Masonite in the middle of a concourse, with CAUTION scribbled on it—directed at nothing in particular, so far as I could tell.

The place was a dump.

And then, Julien became hungry; he wanted a hamburger. But none of the restaurants were open yet. This seemed like a profoundly missed opportunity. Why not generate revenue as well as general interest around the new terminal? Why not allow commerce to take place, *right* before the grand opening—making the tours profitable as well as informative? Julien was pissed off at me for dragging him out to this dead zone where we couldn't even buy a snack. As for myself, I found it refreshing and delightful to wander the terminals with no Bose headphones being hawked, without the universal stench of deep-fried airport food. It felt downright countercultural, to be honest. Like we were all a part of an elaborate flash mob or rogue takeover, repurposing the space at hand for mere ogling.

On that note, though, who deemed it safe to allow thousands of unscreened souls into concourses that will be—in less than two weeks, allegedly—supposedly *secure*? Any number of us could have smuggled guns, explosives, or knives into this space, and hid these things among the prolific building chaos. How did this ridiculously *open* "open house" fit into the black-and-white security protocols that were imminently to be enforced? Was this an actual airport or some sort of absurd replica? It's a point of confusion that I still can't square. Perhaps we're supposed to just not ask. Put our trust in the honor system. I like this idea, in a way. But, then, it's an airport—*if you see something, say something, right?!*

It's possible that the airport was in fact *not* on the verge of opening. After all, the grand opening had been pushed back several times already. Maybe there would be ample time to sweep the concourses for security's sake. But all the airport communications insisted that this is really it: Starting November 6, all flights would depart and arrive into the new terminal.

With regard to the timing, a curious indicator was nestled in the recesses of one of the Starbucks shops that seemed almost on the verge of being open: I noticed Horizon organic milk containers and other drinks in a small cooler in front of the cash register. Those milks would go bad sooner than later. Starbucks seemed certain that the customers were just on the verge of being there. (I found out later from Erin Burns, director of communications for MSY, that the Starbucks shops were in the midst of staff training: thus the products already on set display. Were they real or fake milk bottles? One of the ineffable mysteries of consumer culture.)

A main selling point to the public for the new terminal has been the smorgasbord of restaurant options that will be available—from the local (Midway Pizza, Leah Chase's Place, Sazerac Bar, Cure), to the generic (Chili's, Shake Shack, Panda Express). The local coffee chain PJ's was present, but there was also a California-based Peet's, in addition to the now ubiquitous Starbucks enclaves.

The restaurant facades were bold and brassy, even if they had no burgers to feed Julien on offer yet. It struck me as we walked past the restaurants, with their chairs upside down on the tables and the bars stocked and poised for pouring, what a paradox it is—here especially—to focus on local fare in the terminal. We know it can't be anything other than overpriced simulacra, that

New Orleans airport food is always going be just that: *airport food*. These household names will never live up to their original corollaries in town—they're not supposed to.

The value of the local is strange throughout the new MSY. On the one hand, the airport wants to identify clearly as *our* airport. There is built-in artwork inspired by live oak trees and the Mississippi River—indeed, according to the guide pamphlet, the very architectural design of the building was "influenced by the winding curves" of the river. Likewise, the "dark wood elements in the concourses" are supposed to conjure our place on the planet. But . . . *dark wood*? It doesn't exactly engender any specific regional sentiments, much less precise ecosystems.

During the multiyear construction, there were no open calls for public artworks in the new terminal. The art that's here feels corporate, at best. The center feature of the main terminal is a monolith, an elevator bank adorned with a massive live oak photograph printed on its back—and thus facing the escalators and the first-floor pavilion. On the wall behind the baggage carousels, the curves of a winding river have been imprinted on a metal grid. As far as I could tell, this was where the art started and ended in the new terminal.

Yet there were other unintentional art objects strewn throughout the concourses. Some empty white accessory display or shelf systems in the middle of the concourse resembled mysterious svelte sculptures. Two red mobile lifts were parked askew in a corner, available to look at and ponder. A dark green "2 TON" hoist rested, chains flaccid, behind orange caution tape and with some sort of blanket draped on the ground below—not just left there, but looking almost *positioned*. These were Duchamp-esque readymades: not really meant to be there, not meant to be seen. But there they were, on exhibit.

We walked down the A concourse, which is dedicated to international flights. This arm of the new airport is surprisingly minimalist and utilitarian, bucking the trend of many airports, which go out of their way to spruce up the part of the airport where international flights depart and arrive. The A concourse culminated in Gate 6: a bizarre, Hitchcockian windowless corner of seats. The gate area here seemed—how to say it bluntly?—*forced*. I stood there for a few minutes contemplating the bleak corner and photographing its seating arrangement. Other visitors paused around me to see what I was looking at, but there was nothing really there—*that was the point*.

I sat down to try out the plentiful, uniform airport chairs. One could be excused for mistaking these chairs for the iconic Eames Tandem sling-seats found in many airports around the world; the general topology of these seats has been copied countless times.[1] But the seats in the new MSY are nothing like Eames Tandems. First off, they are rock hard! And, of course, they contain phone chargers at regular intervals, proof that this is an airport of the *twenty-first* century, not the twentieth. The golden age of jet travel, whatever that was for good and ill, is long past. But god help anyone who has to sit in these seats for more than thirty minutes.

I was relishing the oddities sprinkled around the airport, snapping pictures and posting observations to Twitter. Julien, meanwhile, was now both hungry *and* bored. It was time to go.

It was hard not to see the whole building as decidedly generic. As we returned to the main terminal atrium, I couldn't help but recall how I'd felt as a teen in a newly opened supermall in a Detroit suburb in the early 1990s: the *Somerset Collection*.[2] So much open space and natural light—but all for

---

1. https://www.hermanmiller.com/products/seating/lounge-seating/eames-tandem-sling-seating/.
2. https://en.wikipedia.org/wiki/Somerset_Collection.

what? Retail therapy is still therapy—in this case, an attempt to fill an unfillable hole.

It's not clear what is supposed to be illuminated, here in the new airport. Or just what all the empty space in the center of the terminal is meant to accommodate. It was as if the city had gone on a massive retail-therapy binge, resulting in this bright yet empty edifice.

Turning toward the escalators to leave, we heard a few a trumpet notes reverberate across the space—live music was about to happen! Visitors congregated in the Jazz Garden, and a motley assortment of visitors clustered around a few tables on which we saw some aluminum troughs full of snacks. Fritos, Doritos, Lay's potato chips, Nature's Valley granola bars . . . and hundreds of Niagara water bottles being ripped out of their blister packs and lined up on another table. Julien excitedly grabbed a bag of Doritos, and within minutes his fingertips bore that unmistakable orange grime. The Doritos were clearly the highlight of the visit for Julien. This is what it had come to.

As unceremoniously as the tour had begun for us, so it ended. We trundled across the gray pedestrian bridge and back to the car in the cavernous parking garage, Julien looking for a trashcan in which to deposit his empty chip bag. I couldn't help but think about the totally generic snacks on offer back in the terminal. Not a vast platter of powdered sugar–dusted beignets, not to mention oysters—not even Zapp's chips. Just the normal crap you get from Costco in bulk. That water was bottled in a plant outside of Los Angeles, California . . . but who knows where its actual source is. The nonspecific triumphed again. All so we can keep flying, as much and as regularly as possible.

Driving out of the short-term parking garage, we had to consult the small card given to us upon entering. The instructions were deceptively straightforward: Exit toward long-term parking; take a left at the stoplight, drive until it meets Veterans Boulevard. But the way proved meandering and strange. The road turned into rubble, and a police SUV was parked at a roadblock, past which we were waved through by an officer in the driver's seat. Potholes riddled the way. We found ourselves at last on Veterans Boulevard, heading back toward our home in Mid-City. But the trip was prolonged and stop-and-go, as we navigated stoplight after stoplight still without power. It took an hour to get home, as opposed to the normal twenty minutes from the airport. The bookended traffic debacles felt like an omen for the new terminal.

After I'd originally registered for the event online, the instructions for getting to the new airport included a request that I use the hashtag #TheNewMSY when sharing photos and videos of the new terminal: "Photos and videos welcome!" It was clearly intended to be as much of a social-media event as it was staged as a live experience.

Looking back over the hashtag on Twitter later in the day, it seemed as though the downed traffic lights had discouraged many of the would-be visitors from even making it to the new terminal in the first place. Of course the airport staff had no control over the cyclone that morning; but it was surprising that they didn't cancel the event, given the widespread outages and terrible approach circumstances. The airport didn't even mention the traffic snafu on their own Twitter feed. (Probably because power was actually *out* at the old airport across the runway for a better part of the morning, impacting many scheduled flights; the MSY Comms crew surely had enough on their plate already.) The hashtag brought up a few dozen tweets, some praising the new terminal and others complaining about bungled bathroom doors or the missing flyover ramp. It was a little embarrassing that my own ironic tweets crowded the hashtag results.

As I was finishing writing up these notes the following morning, I had to take a break to help my friend Nathan move a willow tree out of my yard and into his friend's truck. Waiting for them to get to my house, I listened and watched as first one, then two, then three Boeing 737s whined by overhead, well into their initial ascents. These mundane flights, another day's departures ticked off one by one, reminded me again of our old airport.

Still very much functioning and mostly fine, the old airport moved people in and out of our region, facilitating the itineraries and cash flows of tourists and locals alike. It was a fine airport, if a bit dingy—and it was about to be relegated to the dustbin of history. Most of it is slated to be demolished, and what remains will supposedly be repurposed as a shipping and private aviation facility. In its place we'll have #TheNewMSY, a bland if Instagrammable airport, dedicated to the future of New Orleans—flyover or no, and with more storms sure to come either way.

How long will the new airport last? Sixty-five years, like its predecessor? With rising sea levels and more frequent storms each year, it's unlikely to be around for more than a couple decades—even though it's blasphemous to admit as much.

For now, the scandal of the missing flyover ramp is the local obsession. In a way it's a handy euphemism for so many problems right now. *Flyover*. As if large groups of people can be summed up because they live in "flyover country." As if a dedicated ramp from the highway leading to the airport would mitigate all the other logistical puzzles and occasional nightmares that commercial flight comprises. As if we can escape our terrestrial life by flying over it, flying away from it. As if flight should ever come easy to our species. As if other organisms, even microbes, can't also *fly*.

On November 19, eleven days after the opening of the new terminal, I headed back out to the airport. This time, I took my five-year-old daughter Camille with me. We were going to meet my parents, who were flying in from Detroit; their plane got in at 5:30 p.m. or so, and we were hoping to find some dinner and explore the terminal before they arrived.

The highway was a little backed-up a few miles from the airport exit, but this seemed to have more to do with rush hour commuters heading home from downtown and less to do with airport traffic. Exiting, I was prepared for the worst—but we coasted up to the stoplight and were the only car waiting to turn. The absent flyover was like a fading nightmare.

I could see how the three stoplights would likely get choked up during high-volume periods, but all in all the route was direct and easy. By the time we were centrifuging the roundabouts, it all seemed planned and tidy. As we approached the terminal, Camille blurted out, "Look at that *ramp!*" She was describing the minimal architectural flare that rises off the end of the international concourse—it's the triangular roofline swooping above the windowless corner at the end of the A gates that had confounded me, when I was inside during the open house. And Camille was right: it looked like a little ramp to nowhere.

The past eleven days had seen checked baggage computer glitches, ground transportation gridlocks, and punishingly long security lines. A couple jet bridges were reported broken as planes arrived, requiring gate changes and minor delays. Screeds were published in the local paper, and a few angry Twitter threads unspooled. But, overall, the transition went pretty smoothly. I could see now that everything had, somewhat miraculously, fallen into place.

We took our parking ticket and ascended the short-term garage. (The first half hour is free!) After finding a spot, we headed toward the walkway to the terminal. Entering on the third level, I was again struck by the compactness of the check-in area. Camille was delighted by the array of escalators and wanted to ride them all.

I had looked up our dining options before we left and knew there was the Peet's Coffee on the third level, and Parish Provisions on the first level, near the baggage claim. Neither of these was a restaurant per se, but I figured we could get *something* decent between the two venues. It was #TheNewMSY, after all!

I noticed a giant STEM-themed banner advertising the University of New Orleans above the check-in lobby—a missed opportunity for my school; Loyola will probably just get a little poster in the baggage claim area, like we had in the old airport.

The airport already seemed like it'd been there forever. Passengers pulled weathered roller bags through the terminal, chauffeurs with name signs were slouched on benches in the arrivals area, and security officers zipped around on those three-wheeled standing scooters, looking ridiculous.

After wandering the three levels for a bit, we ended up back at the Peet's: I ordered a ham and Swiss sandwich, and a cup of dark roast. ("That's all we have," said the woman behind the counter.) We headed back two long escalators to the Parish Provisions, where Camille selected a premade, soggy-looking PB&J. We bought a bottled water with a smiley face emoji on the packaging. It grinned at us as we sat in the baggage claim area, on benches (no chairs or tables in sight), and ate our pathetic dinner. The performance stage nearby was empty; no band was playing for arriving passengers. The place was already getting dirty: black streaks from roller bags dragged sideways marred the white tile flooring.

Bags started appearing the carousel behind us and my parents arrived, looking no more or no less travel weary than usual. Leaving the airport was smooth; no hold-ups.

Everything was fine.

The airport quickly achieved something like normalcy. There would be a few hiccups later, having to do with checked baggage computers and the like, but all in all the new terminal was a staggering success, bringing in record numbers of tourists and visitors over the initial months of operation.

My mother had brought me a magazine page ripped carefully out of an *Architectural Digest,* which featured an interior photograph of the newest Beijing airport, Daxing International.[3] It looked like a rendering, sans passengers or even any airline workers for that matter. It vaguely resembled the new MSY—if much bigger. Looking at this image, it occurred to me that terminals look great without people. There's a strange gap between what we want airports to be, absent travelers, and what they *are,* when they become operational—even at their best.

When my friend Mark headed out to the new airport for the first time the following week, to pick up a family member around Thanksgiving, he sent me a photograph that he took inside the terminal, of a sign near the security checkpoint. It said: "You are your ID." That summed it up. Airports might work better if we really *were* just our IDs. No bomb-carrying (or virus-harboring) bodies. No attitudes, no risk factors. Just numbers, sheer data, for the safety of everyone. Perhaps the missing flyover at the new MSY is an unconscious extension of this logic—maybe it's not *missing* at all. It may sound outlandish, but what if the optimal airport was not overly concerned with the conveyance of actual human bodies? If anything, maybe human bodies just get in the way of the real goal: the unimpeded accumulation of capital. And if humans stopped needing to fly or suddenly stopped taking to the skies—what then?

3. https://www.architecturaldigest.com/story/inside-beijings -daxing-international-airport-terminal-by-zaha-hadid.

The 30,000-Foot View

HOW MANY MEETINGS have I been in where an administrator, manager, or executive holds forth on "what things look like from 30,000 feet"? It's an expression that is meant to suggest a zoomed-out assessment, the perspective of a supervisor who can see everything. Or, if not *everything,* at least more than the peons who are at ground level. It's meant to convey authority, and it is also a plea for trust: *I can see more than you—trust me, do as I say.*

This is not the Romantic ideal of the cloud's-eye view, as imagined in the poetry of Wordsworth and Shelley in the nineteenth century.[1] And neither is it the carceral viewpoint of the Panopticon, as articulated by Bentham and later famously drawn out by Foucault.[2] No, the 30,000-foot view is an especially contemporary formulation.

These days we might be tempted to associate the aerial view more with drones or satellite views. Surveillance, global information systems, and even death administered from above—all in

1. https://www.poetryfoundation.org/poems/45521/i-wandered-lonely-as-a-cloud and https://www.poetryfoundation.org/poems/45117/the-cloud-56d2247bf4112.
2. https://www.jstor.org/stable/25594995?seq=1#page_scan_tab_contents.

the form of data delivered to our smartphones or to government war rooms. Of course satellites are way higher than 30,000 feet and operate on an entirely different modality of seeing. And drones, for all their increasing ubiquity, are more likely to be experienced in the home (as remote-control toys), or above the workplace, recreational zone, or private property while capturing digital imagery (e.g., for an ad spot, social-media feed, or real-estate listing).

But the 30,000-foot view comes from a more ordinary perspective: it is a byproduct of the cruising vantage point of the commercial airliner that is constantly traveling at this height, everywhere and always. Go outside and look up, and within five minutes you're likely to see a set of contrails come into view. Right there is the 30,000-foot perspective—and it's moving fast. Some of those glints in the sky might be military planes, but for the most part they are the Boeings and Airbuses making their innumerable daily schlepps across the globe.

To see things from 30,000 feet is a more palatable metaphor, then, because it's a view that so many business travelers and vacationers have seen, if only in a passing and disinterested fashion. It's the bland view from above, demilitarized, anaesthetized— even verging on *boring*. Who hasn't sat in a cramped window seat and gazed out at unfurling agricultural grids below, or undulating snowcapped peaks, or endless ocean waters . . . and merely sighed? But the rhetorical trick in this expression is that the 30,000-foot view is imbued with something greater for those who can *read* it, for those who can *control* it. And by control, I don't mean to *pilot*.

The 30,000-foot view is meant to achieve multiple effects: it is supposed to connote a particular scale (of planning, oversight) and wonder—a sense of awe in the total work of whatever is ostensibly being viewed. These multiple effects are bundled together in the expression and mutually reinforce each other.

As Caren Kaplan puts it in her book *Aerial Aftermaths,* "Aerial imagery is popularly believed to provide the ultimate objective representation."[3] This view stands for the knowledge of someone (or some higher entity) who can see *more.* And this view is never neutral. It immediately produces power over the people over whom such a position is wielded. The 30,000-foot view is rarely evoked outside of an economic structure wherein workers are struggling to sustain a system or implement a new strategy, while a boss or outside consultant urges them on—often on the precipice of financial ruin.

For example, in a recent book called *The Polymath: Unlocking the Power of Human Versatility,* Waqas Ahmed quotes Tim Ferriss (self-help guru and author of *The 4-Hour Workweek: Escape 9–5, Live Anywhere, and Join the New Rich*) employing this expression: "Taking the 30-thousand foot view helps you to look at the interrelatedness and interconnectedness of different fields as opposed to viewing them as purely separate disciplines." This is no mere description of how a certain pulled-back perspective functions philosophically and transdisciplinarily. Rather, it serves for Ahmed as part of an assessment of "highly successful entrepreneurs and investors."[4] In other words, the 30,000-foot view is not about knowledge for knowledge's sake, but about calculation and speculation. It's about maximizing profit.

The 30,000-foot view summons a graspable, ordinary vantage point (at least in contemporary consumer society) in order to immediately rarify it. The people who know what to *do* with this view are to be listened to and obeyed. Sure, everyone in an airplane gets a 30,000-foot view. But those in first class are the

3. Caren Kaplan, *Aerial Aftermaths: Wartime from Above* (Durham, N.C.: Duke University Press, 2018).

4. Waqas Ahmend, *The Polymath: Unlocking the Power of Human Versatility* (Hoboken, N.J.: Wiley, 2019).

ones who can use this expression tactically, in the right moments, to make organizational decisions—investments or cuts, mergers or downsizing, promotions or layoffs.

While everyone is (in theory) invited to see things from 30,000 feet, not everyone is invited to stay there, or to make decisions from such an elevated position. The expression is then a sinister double maneuver, a promise of *sharing* knowledge while also an act of *restricting* power. It works this way: "Here's how things look from 30,000 feet. Can you see? Good, now I am going to make a unilateral decision based on this. There is no room for negotiation, because I have shown you how things look, so you must understand." The totalizing picture is captured and conveyed in the spirit of transparency, but always with the ulterior motive of exerting and protecting a reified point of authority.

Even if we hesitate before such an outright critique of the economic structure underlying this expression, there are more fundamental problems with the 30,000-foot view: Its specific scalar shift makes no sense, and the perspective is utterly askew.

The scale intended to be communicated by the 30,000-foot view is more accurately understood by the architectural plan or the exploded view of how a machine's parts fit together. By looking at the components of a complicated organism or organization, decisions can be made about individual segments or that will affect the whole. But this is clearly not attained by a 30,000-foot view in any literal sense. In fact, what one gets from looking out an airplane window is more often a sense of bewildering vastness, of the ongoingness of terrain below. Viewing an urban center from so high is no less dizzying; even if one can orient on the grid and identify familiar landmarks or buildings, such a view does not necessarily synthesize a total picture so much as reveal just how elaborate and intricate such a cityscape is.

And often at 30,000 feet, it's just clouds.

Then there is the matter of perspective. Looking out an airplane window rarely affords a top-down view. More often than not, the angle of perception is oblique and fragmented, resulting in an indistinct tableau. Seeing things from 30,000 feet hardly translates to an intact, discrete picture of a place or region, because commercial air travel is not oriented in this way—glass-bottomed airliners are still a fantasy, at least for now.[5] Interestingly, seatback screens with "flight tracker" technology offer a version of this visualization, whereby passengers can zoom in and out as they fly over land and sea. But even then, this view is not about assessing the whole in order to make strategic determinations; rather, it's a form of in-flight entertainment, and it is largely passive.

Given the illogical nature of the expression, why do we still proffer advice from the 30,000-foot view? Perhaps it has something to do with our collective, cultural investment in air travel as a sort of pinnacle of modernity—and a belief in perpetual flight. Even though commercial airliners offer no such view on things below, the promise of achieving a certain class status coincident with frequent flight retains a strong allure. To be able to claim the view from 30,000 feet is not about making an objective assessment so much as it is about proclaiming (however vaguely) one's net worth—and thus one's ability to make respected (and final) decisions.

What presents itself as having the sheen of objectivity turns out to mask the inescapably subjective nature of leadership and decision making. Subjective, and jealously individualistic. The view from 30,000 feet is precisely the one that *I* am going to explain to you, in order to situate and justify *my* actions—actions that will impact those over whom I am in a position of power.

5. https://www.virgin.com/richard-branson/virgin-launches-glass-bottomed-plane.

Strangely, it's not about flight at all; rather, this vertical metaphor works to reinforce horizontal power dynamics between individuals.

Or if it is about flight, it's not so much about seeing what's out the window as it is about keeping the very concept of "first class" coveted, even sacred. Our god's-eye view may be more modest in some ways than the ancient depictions of such a perspective—set only at 30,000 feet—but in other ways the quantities of wealth and power that get consolidated under this view are more than even the most fantastical Xanadu could have ever contained.

The Flying-V

IF WE HAVE BECOME inured to aviation metaphors as slimy business-speak, then it's no wonder that we're so desperate for any sign of good news from the sky, any hint that things are getting better up in the clouds and on the runways.

After a tough year in aviation in 2018—the grounding of the 737 MAX after two fatal crashes,[1] the crashing of airline computer systems across the United States,[2] the announcement of the end of the superjumbo A380[3]—in 2019 we needed some good news about commercial flight. And that summer, the good news arrived in the form of a revolutionary future airliner.

In early June 2019, CNN swooned over the story of an innovative airplane design called the Flying-V, which was being funded by the Amsterdam-based KLM.[4] This was to be an air-

1. https://www.washingtonpost.com/business/boeings-grounded
-737-max-the-story-so-far/2019/05/05/22d6db04-6fa4-11e9-9331
-30bc5836f48e_story.html.

2. https://www.vox.com/the-goods/2019/3/26/18282767/sabre
-outage-american-airlines-jetblue-alaska-delays.

3. https://www.theguardian.com/business/2019/feb/14/a380
-airbus-to-end-production-of-superjumbo.

4. https://www.cnn.com/travel/article/klm-flying-v-plane-scli-intl
/index.html.

liner with a titillating new shape, summed up by its eponymous letter. According to early reports, the Flying-V would match the capacity of current widebody jetliners such as the A350 and Boeing 787, but with a twist. The new plane proposed a novel experience of commercial flight: Two aisles running down two separate fuselages which comprise the wings themselves (never mind that half the window seats will *not* be. Instead, a wall will be there; claustrophobic travelers beware).

The idea of a V-shaped plane is not exactly new, but KLM has indicated fresh interest in making this geometry the vanguard in commercial flight.[5] Notably, the Flying-V promises greater fuel efficiency by harnessing "synergy" between the wings and the body of the plane. Outlets from *Boing Boing*[6] and *Travel + Leisure*[7] to *Maxim*[8] latched onto this story, quoting and re-quoting copy and recycling striking illustrations of the concept plane—as if it were already hooked up to a jet bridge and ready for passengers. Ready to fly.

But there's a curious thing about the Flying-V. All this buzz around a futuristic aircraft really is not about transportation goals, much less a revolution in commercial aviation. Rather, the Flying-V is a totem of the *Anthropocene*—our current turning point in geological history, an inflection defined by destructive human impact.[9]

5. https://newatlas.com/go/7694/.

6. https://boingboing.net/2019/06/03/klm-funds-new-flying-v-pla.html.

7. https://www.travelandleisure.com/airlines-airports/klm-airlines-developing-flying-v-passenger-plane.

8. https://www.maxim.com/gear/new-gibson-guitar-inspired-jet-2019-6.

9. https://www.theguardian.com/environment/2019/may/30/anthropocene-epoch-have-we-entered-a-new-phase-of-planetary-history.

Even the casual reader cannot miss how the reporting of the Flying-V was consistently framed around a frantic desire for the *sustainability* of commercial flight. Every article highlighted how the new aircraft promises up to 20 percent greater fuel efficiency, and multiple articles noted global CO_2 emissions by way of celebrating the new design. The subtext of all this reporting was that air travel as we knew it wreaks havoc on the environment. The Flying-V stories were like a classic instance of literary apophasis: *I'm NOT going to tell you how bad for the environment our old airliners are.* . . . The bad effects are evident from the interruption of bird and insect migration routes, to carbon emissions in the atmosphere and voracious fossil fuel consumption. Front-page news items about the Flying-V all but admit that air travel is exorbitantly wasteful, and all but certainly reaching a crisis point.

And yet, in these stories commercial flight also seems paradoxically determined to metastasize.

The story of the Flying-V turns out to be fixated on an alternative present, even as it alleges to be about a sustainable future form of flight, in "20 to 30 years." As such, this imaginary airplane is also about our inability to conceptualize the Anthropocene as a real problem that we must engage *right now*. And not just through a technological quick fix or slight adjustment to an existing situation. Rather, the Anthropocene requires humans on a large scale to respond radically, through an entire realignment of how our species understands itself and interacts with the planet and its myriad other inhabitants.

Given the realities of commercial aircraft these days—the stubborn rivalry of the twin workhorses the Airbus A320 and the Boeing 737; the trembling of the still-grounded 737 MAX (not coincidentally also sold on a promise of greater fuel efficiency); the end of jumbo jets; the elusive return of supersonic travel on a mass scale—we have reason to be seriously skeptical of any venture that would significantly change the shape of commercial aircraft. Commercial air travel as we know it is too entrenched and is settling down ever deeper into a sheer monotype: twin-engine airliners, small-to-medium size, geared to worldwide productivity. Costs and time of retraining are prohibitive factors to any serious reimagining of flight.

And speaking of costs: The fine print of the Flying-V news went on to explain that this isn't a "new plane" at all—at least, not yet. Rather, the reality is that a certain large company (KLM) was funding research and design for *the idea* of a new plane. The verb *funding* was key, and why some environmental thinkers prefer the name *Capitalocene* for our current epoch: this name puts a point on the fantasy of vast amounts of capital accumulated by multinational conglomerates or powerful sole owners, capital that then might be channeled in *just the right way,* as if to magically and precisely fix the problems borne by modernity.[10]

Of course, capital doesn't work like this, as if it can jump the future or snap its fingers and get something done at once (build a wall, invent a new plane, provide Wi-Fi for all, go to Mars). No, capital spreads out but gets unevenly distributed; it exploits many people while elevating a very few. Capital builds on itself but not with any other goal in mind. Capital doesn't care about sustainability but only about amassing frantically, while it can. Or put another way, while air travel is concerned with real origins and destinations, capital doesn't need to go *anywhere* in order to develop. Maybe it doesn't even need a world at all.

Finally, we must talk about the name: *Flying-V*. This appellation, referencing a Gibson "Flying-V" electric guitar, aestheticizes the airplane—and renders the whole enterprise akin to glam entertainment. The name conjures Lenny Kravitz, or maybe Eddie Van Halen, at some epic show in the past. As if this is all

10. https://www.tandfonline.com/doi/abs/10.1080/03066150.2016.1235036.

just a flashy rock concert, a mass spectacle that we might wake up from tomorrow morning, hung over and saying what a great time it was. And in a sense, it was.

As another piece of mere clickbait—a brief piece of quasi-news that circulated online for a day or two, something to be distracted by for a few minutes, forward on to a friend or two, sneer at or be amazed by—the Flying-V story becomes part of the Anthropocene in another way. It is evidence of the weirdly timeless drift of the internet, the lazy yet relentless expansion of circuits and devices, nodes and wires, screens and buttons, satellites and cell towers: all the infrastructure and apparatus that pins us to this place and time while we simultaneously confront the horror of a horizon past which all these things will become obsolete, the internet a fading memory of a past of seeming plenty. Where we cataloged all our hopes and fears, where we even stored our airplanes of the future, airplanes that would show that we'd learned and adjusted our behaviors to live more sensitively in the world.

But it turned out we were only hastening the world's end as we knew it, by insisting that everything remain the same . . . even as we thought we were planning a better future way of flying, of living.

Dwell Time

WHEN I TEACH my "Interpreting Airports" seminar at Loyola University New Orleans, we often discuss how *time* is a funny thing at airports. When your departure gets delayed, thirty minutes can feel like an eternity. When you're running late to catch a flight and navigating the interiors of an international terminal, an hour can go by in the blink of an eye. The security line inches along excruciatingly until you're at the checkpoint, and then you suddenly feel rushed, tripping over your shoes as you strip down and plunder your own bags for X-ray screening.

One reliable thing to do with extra (even unwanted) time at the airport is to eat. Lately, airport food has been trying to outgrow its connotations as bland and generic; I've seen this most clearly in our brand-new airport in New Orleans, where the new terminal boasts favorite local eateries and bars featuring signature dishes and special drinks for passengers to enjoy before they depart or after they arrive—when the airport finally opened, these venues received (mostly) rave reviews. The airport even developed a limited "guest pass" system, whereby nontraveling locals could pass through security just to dine.

In an article about the array of restaurants at the new MSY, I noticed a curiously technical phrase used to describe how the concessioners approached these venues: "Airport restaurateurs have to learn the dynamics of 'dwell time' (the time passengers spend at the terminal)."[1] *Dwell time* means estimating and capturing potential customers in their element: not necessarily as diners first and foremost, but as travelers. *Dwelling* runs counter to the fundamental logic of airports, which is to keep people *flowing*.

But "dwell time" has another meaning, for another domain of contemporary culture: website design and management. Dwell time can also refer to how many seconds, minutes, or even hours users spend on a single webpage. As one digital marketing company defines it, "Dwell time combines a certain amount of art and science to the internet experience. It's a measure of how your users utilize your website by factoring in how long they hang out on certain pages."[2] Lingering on a web page also means seeing ads and potentially clicking on them (on purpose or by accident), thus directing corresponding revenue flows to the advertisers.

At first blush, these two uses of dwell time may sound similar enough. They each suggest an attention to how long people stay in a place (in an airport, on a website), and they are both aimed at maximizing revenue. But in an important way, the different uses of the phrase have oppositional purposes: Dwell time in airports is a critically temporary and fleeting interval. Online, dwell time might be maximized in the moment, but ideally drawn out perpetually. An app or website can only hope that such time spent there continues and becomes all-consuming. The dream of dwell time in an online sense is that it might become *all* the time. That the user never clicks away. The longer the time the user is on the site, the more revenue streams back toward the

1. https://www.nola.com/entertainment_life/eat-drink/article_caa0daa6-fccb-11e9-977d-3fe8c7242366.html.
2. https://zerogravitymarketing.com/what-is-dwell-time/.

host. Imagine the social media that never gets turned off, akin to the interactive operating system in Spike Jonze's 2013 film *Her*.

In both usages, "dwell time" is a euphemism for revenue potential, an opportunity to extract profit. But whereas the airport example is spatialized and temporized in physically contained senses, internet dwell time is able to insinuate itself into so many other places and moments of everyday life. Yet fascinatingly, in airports the two forms of dwell time occasionally coexist and overlap. Picture a delayed traveler eating fries or sipping a beer while idly scrolling through their Instagram or Facebook feed. *Waiting, dwelling, consuming.*

But the commingling of these two forms of dwell time has a limit. Airports must keep passengers moving: from waiting to departing, from arrivals to baggage and curbside, and eventually back again. Dwell time is temporary, bounded, and cyclical. Dwell time on one's phone or computer, on the other hand, can precede—and extend through and beyond—the airport. Ideally, online dwell time is even maintained throughout the stages of flight: on-board Wi-Fi increasingly makes this possible (and even *expected*, as we noted earlier).

The conjunction of these two forms of dwell time can create an unnerving sight. A few years ago, airport restaurants began installing iPads on which customers could order their food and drink—and into which they could gaze, scrolling and tapping, while they waited for and then consumed their items. Every traveler a modern Narcissus.

Encountering these spaces for the first time could be an uncanny experience: the disappeared wait staff, the compulsory media saturation, the aura of total tablet domination. Looking at these spaces through the double lens of dwell time, the image is even more unsettling. Travelers appear reduced to livestock, equally stationed in front of uniform digital troughs and overpriced veggie wraps.

This increasingly common airport scene, seen slightly aslant, might call to mind the Wachowskis' 1999 film *The Matrix,* when we first realize where Neo has been living his whole life: in a cubical-like, life-supporting vat. Neo is plugged in, thoroughly satiated and entertained by an elaborate simulation. Dwell time is all the time, for Neo—until he breaks free from the matrix.

We may not be worried about getting stuck in the airport, interpellated into such a stark cyberpunk scene. We like to think we can get in and out of airplanes and airports decisively and without ambiguity. We may feel as though our phones and computers are still in our hands, so to speak—that we can control where we dwell, and for how long. We know when to shut our computers down for the night, when to put our phones into airplane mode.

But if we run these spiral-bound scenarios out to their logical conclusions—which is what capitalism tends to do: to *grow* growth, to metastasize—we can see how the situation becomes uncomfortably blurry. Internet commerce desires as much dwell time as possible. Airports don't necessarily need dwell time to increase at airport restaurants for discrete passengers. Rather, airports work to facilitate sufficient—if not constant—dwell time in their restaurants as part of a larger effort to maintain the flow of departures and arrivals. In other words, optimized dwell time at the airport requires human transit to remain perpetual. We might not yet recognize our flying selves in Keanu Reeves's captive Neo from *The Matrix,* but with commercial air travel on the rise and persona digital media technologies only proliferating . . . there will only be more opportunities to collapse the boundaries between varying forms of dwell time.

In this light, it's interesting to ponder how none other than Keanu Reeves has come to embody a particularly mesmerizing form of dwell time, as an unquenchable internet meme.[3] So much

3. https://giphy.com/explore/keanu-reeves.

so that *any* Keanu news or sighting becomes something to follow, something to dwell on. One doesn't even need to create a meme: Keanu comes readymade, even to the point of becoming the unmistakable voice of Duke Caboom in *Toy Story 4*. For some ineffable reason, Keanu has become the perfect thing to look at bemusedly, between other clicks and views. As if we might dwell with Keanu, forever in flight with his magisterial visage.

Ode to Empty Airports

REMEMBER WHEN I visited the empty New Orleans airport? Well, it was empty of *travelers,* anyway. During that open house I still remember glancing over at the new consolidated security checkpoint as we walked through the parallel hallway—X-ray machines half-assembled, shrink-wrapped body scanners lying on the floor. I recall thinking that the security checkpoint was going to get choked during holiday travel periods. What I didn't anticipate was that the security checkpoint might in fact become empty again all too soon, for very different reasons.

A funny thing about that open house was how pleasant it was. At one point Julien and I ran into some friends from his school and chatted with them for a while. People were ambling about unhurriedly, marveling at the restaurants not yet open and trying out the new seats in their familiar rows. People gazed out the plate-glass windows at the tarmac—no airplanes in the immediate vicinity. This wasn't an airport empty of *people* but empty of *flight*. And it seemed to be almost better for it.

In early 2020, as news of the novel coronavirus spread, we began to see occasional photographs of empty airports in different parts of the world. Then abruptly in the images changed dramatically: they became pictures of jam-packed terminals,[1]

1. https://www.wsj.com/articles/passengers-returning-from

snaking lines representing the terrifying "superspreader" potential of the virus.[2] Air travel was being massively disrupted as people rushed to get home, before travel was further restricted and borders closed, before flights were canceled. Teeming with frantic passengers and chaos one week, the following week found airports quite empty once again, a different kind of disorder.

Think of the last time you had a perfect flight experience.

You probably breezed through security without having to wait even a minute. Your departure gate was uncrowded, and when you needed to plug in your phone, you had your choice of a dozen outlets in the vicinity. Boarding went so fast that the plane was ready to leave a few minutes early; you even had a whole row to yourself. The flight attendants lavished you with drinks and snacks, cracking jokes about the not even half-full plane. The captain, too, remarked over the intercom on how the skies were even friendlier than normal, with the plane so empty. Deplaning was relaxed, and the terminal on the other end of the journey was equally tranquil—almost a ghost town, but not in a haunting way. Your rental car keys were waiting for you, and you sped away from the airport a successful and thoroughly appeased modern passenger.

The sight of an empty airport can offer the promise of a smooth trip. But empty airports lately have portended something very different: the wholesale shuddering of this vast, elaborate enterprise called flight.

This state of affairs was made vivid by photographs of empty airports accompanying coronavirus-themed headlines—perhaps most chillingly at *The Atlantic* with an article titled "Cancel

-abroad-face-long-crowded-lines-at-airports-11584276068.

2. http://news.mit.edu/2012/spread-of-disease-in-airports-0723.

Everything."[3] The novel coronavirus took a toll on the commercial aviation sector, spurring airlines to ground planes, curb their economic outlooks, accommodate swells of itinerary cancellations and changes, and plead for passengers to remain loyal through these turbulent times. Meanwhile, the federal government doled a massive bailout to the airlines for the whole fiasco.

In a March 9 email to SkyMiles members, Delta CEO Ed Bastian stated that "travel is fundamental to our business and our lives, which is why it can't—and shouldn't—simply stop." It was a subtle but shrewd move, this lumping together of *can't* and *shouldn't,* therein leaving open the troubling possibility of either/or. Because of course air travel already *had* stopped in many regions around the globe, from many flights in the United Kingdom and Europe[4] to a slew of flights going in and out of Australia,[5] even as passengers still hurried to get back home, wherever that was for them.

Any other time we might have welcomed the quietude descending on these raucous social nodes. Air travel is often the worst for passengers when it's busiest: cramped aircraft cabins, long lines at check-in or security, the exhausted scrum of baggage claim during peak travel times. . . . When it's empty, or nearly so, an airport can inspire sensations of individual freedom and mobility unparalleled. The vaulted ceilings feel even higher, and the airplanes all seem there just for you.

The empty airport, then, has a strange doubleness to it. Such a space can represent the wish image of air travel: a personal-

---

3. https://www.theatlantic.com/ideas/archive/2020/03 /coronavirus-cancel-everything/607675/.

4. https://www.bbc.com/news/business-51904769.

5. https://www.theguardian.com/world/2020/mar/18/australian -airlines-offer-credit-for-cancelled-flights-as-routes-slashed-amid -coronavirus.

ized adventure, the individuated feeling of being spirited up and across a continent or ocean with no apparent obstacles. But a deserted security checkpoint can also signify something quite different. It underscores the baseline fragility and collectivity of our interconnected and networked world, where something as small and site-specific as a novel virus can travel fast and thereby ensnarl—and threaten to terminate—the whole system.

One of the more horrifying stories to circulate over those early weeks of the pandemic had to do with so called "ghost flights," or how airlines were flying empty planes on their routes in order to keep their takeoff and landing spots at coveted airports.[6] While some airports sat uncomfortably desolate on the ground, corollary empty jetliners whizzed far above. This particular practice was quickly called into question and in some cases halted, but still countless planes flew mostly empty through the skies as the last travelers raced home. Right at the time that I was originally writing about this, my university issued a statement prohibiting all faculty and staff from international travel as well as all "official non-crucial domestic air travel" until further notice. We were effectively grounded.

Amid all this, the Delta website posted a new page dedicated to "Six ways Delta is supporting healthy flying."[7] A list of "proactive and voluntary steps" covered the basics of personal hygiene and collective well-being necessary for this moment. An architectural rendering of a modern terminal appeared at the top of the page, generic travelers looking unconcerned and

6. https://www.citylab.com/transportation/2020/03/coronavirus-airline-travel-ghost-flights-empty-planes/607624/.
7. https://news.delta.com/6-ways-delta-supporting-healthy-flying.

on their way. There were no signs of the COVID-19 pandemic in this fictive, robust airport.

Yet the spectral empty airports, slapdash travel bans, and consuming ghost planes all raised serious questions: What if flying was not healthy, period? What if we were discovering, through this drawn-out period of uncertainty, that air travel on the magnitude that we have achieved is riddled with unhealthy, disastrous side effects?

In all the empty airports a rift was exposed: between humble continuance and sheer economic growth. Air travel could potentially be calibrated to a more modest level that would be less ecologically destructive and make it easier to stem future outbreaks. But airlines and airports are driven by a model of constant expansion such that *any* decrease in flights is immediately felt as a loss (and a staggering loss, in this case). The empty airport became a sort of zero level of this dilemma, signifying the deep contradiction within modern flight. Given certain circumstances, such as the spread of the novel coronavirus, this form of transportation was not just shown to be unsustainable but was abandoned in a flash: Its voracious capacity is its very downfall.

President Trump's belated call for Americans to keep gatherings to ten people or less effectively shut down commercial flight: It was impossible to conceive of airport lines or cost-effective airliners operating under that dictum.[8] And no matter the magnitude of governmental aid, air travel would not easily bounce back; a reckoning was happening.

What could we do with empty airports? How could we re-inhabit these spaces, once the novel coronavirus has run its course? These questions are very much open, for now.

8. https://www.politico.com/news/2020/03/16/trump -recommends-avoiding-gatherings-of-more-than-10-people-132323.

Climate activist Greta Thunberg brought our attention to the folly of air travel and its significant role in our planetary predicament. But politicians, pundits, and frequent travelers could brush off a lone teen easily enough. Now in the ongoing time of COVID-19, we are being forced to pause and seriously reconsider this modality of transit, commercial flight and all its spoils.

Grounded

AMONG THOSE old enough to remember it, it was common to hear that the pandemic recalled the feeling of 9/11 and the weeks that followed. One could sense this especially in the quietude of the skies: There were far fewer commercial airliners flying overhead early in the pandemic, just like there were then, in the days after the terrorist attacks. The lack of contrails was noticeable, even if you were not in the habit of noticing them ordinarily. At the still sparkling new airport outside New Orleans, nearly all outbound flights were canceled on the morning that I started writing this chapter.

As a one news story reported, commercial flight had "sunk to a level not seen in more than 60 years."[1] Obviously this wasn't due to the vagaries of consumer demand or the emergence of a better way to travel: People weren't flying in order to keep the coronavirus from taking more lives. They weren't flying because there's nowhere they were supposed to go but home.

The human cost of the pandemic far outweighs the fate of the aviation industry. But aviation is also an index of certain common aspirations, such as professional mobility, vacation travel, and

1. https://www.politico.com/news/2020/03/16/trump
-recommends-avoiding-gatherings-of-more-than-10-people-132323.

social connection. With flight, there was always a physically transcendent factor: the push into your seat on takeoff, the breath held right before touching down. The ideals of progress could be felt in the body and as a kind of euphoria as the plane punched through clouds.

As people stopped flying, vast fleets were grounded around the world. Planes were parked in carefully staggered rows on tarmacs, raked wings tessellating as these mechanical birds lay dormant. What few travelers there were would post photos to their social media feeds of barren concourses and unoccupied gate areas, airplane cabins hauntingly vacant. Complimentary drinks felt very different when no one else was around.

With the majority of airliners grounded and airports all but deserted, the persistent wish images of commercial flight over the past seventy years seemed like relics of another epoch. In 1950, Northwest Airlines called their coast-to-coast Stratocruiser a "Castle in the air!" And since the dawn of the jet age, fantasies of airborne cosmopolitanism had reigned supreme. As one Pan Am transatlantic ad from 1959 put it, "*Halfway to Europe between cocktails and coffee.*" Promoting the supersonic Concorde, British Airways would roll out an ad in the 1980s with this mouthful: "Who cares enough to make the world half as big by flying twice as fast? We care!"

In the ebbs and flows of airline ad campaigns across these years, what stands out is how the glamor of flying was always set against its increased accessibility. In other words, the experience of flight was at once rarified and democratized—a delicate balancing act. For instance, in the early 1970s, American Airlines announced their opulent coach lounge on the Boeing 747 with the claim that "You won't believe you're on an airplane"—an apparent acknowledgment of flying's cramped inconvenience. By the late '70s, TWA was punning on the spaciousness of their latest widebody airliners, which evinced "not a crowd in the sky."

Flying was both a luxury and not luxurious enough, a way to join the crowd and at the same time try to escape it.

This alchemy became a common theme. In an aesthetic that now seems eerily prescient, so many early airline ads featured near empty planes, with one passenger or a romantic couple marveling at all the space around them. In 2020 we found similar snapshots being shared, but the travelers in these interiors were unsettled: Planes aren't supposed to be this empty, even if that was always the fantasy.[2]

The space and privilege of business and first class were always dependent on the steady scrunch of an economy class. Flight attendants would hand out pamphlets for loyalty cards, offering the key to better service—if glossing the brute realities of the economic hustle involved therein. Signing up for a frequent flier program is one thing; attaining Diamond status requires a significant financial commitment. To borrow a term from theorist Sarah Sharma, we might say that the "temporal architecture" of air travel is meted out in inches and points, armrests and miles.[3] It's a race that anyone can join but that no one ever wins. In a certain sense, modern air travel had become as much about the status and privilege enjoyed en route as actually going places.

This glamor survived and persisted beyond 9/11, newly imbued with patriotic symbolism and a collective sense of entitlement— as though air travel had emerged as a quintessentially American right. Within a few years air travel was ramping back up, planes voraciously gobbling up and spewing out passengers around the world again. The perceived dangers in flying were addressed by more elaborate screening measures: Full-body scanners were

2. https://www.nytimes.com/2020/03/26/travel/coronavirus -empty-planes.html.

3. Sarah Sharma, *In the Meantime: Temporality and Cultural Politics* (Durham, N.C.: Duke University Press, 2014).

deployed, and travelers started taking off their shoes when passing through security checkpoints. People learned to travel with small bottles of shampoos and conditioners. It's not yet clear what measures will be put in place to make flying seem safe from viral transmission—or if such measures will work.

During the first two decades of the twenty-first century, even as commercial flight bloomed again, frayed edges were also showing around the whole organism. Airlines squeezed seats closer together, even in first class. Checked baggage charges were invented practically overnight, creating a new revenue stream for airlines if also annoyingly clogging overhead bins, complicating the flight crew's jobs, and creating headaches for weary passengers. Boeing hurried to produce a new mass-market version of the 737, the unfortunately named "MAX," which resulted in at least two fatal crashes. (When Donald Trump spoke of helping out Boeing as part of the coronavirus relief, he hinted at how the airplane manufacturer was already beleaguered by the stain of the MAX—as if it made sense that the pandemic should brush that other problem under the rug.)

Still, during this time more travelers than ever flocked to the sky each year, as commercial flight grew ever more common and expected. In 2013, United Airlines brought back its "Fly the friendly skies" slogan—a reboot of commercial-aviation idealism from forty years prior. This constancy belied a subtle shift, though. We have come a long way from the glamor assumed in early commercial flight. Travelers have become numb to the gritty determination and grind of the post-9/11 journey, with its uniformed security regime, encouraged paranoia ("If you see something, say something!"), and squabbles over seatback reclines and personal device volume. Recording incidents of "air rage" became a social media pastime. Democracy on an airliner was always a highly ambivalent thing. But no one thought it would end so abruptly.

As in air, so too on the ground. The quick plummet of flight's utility may prove to be eerily indicative of a broader dynamic, in which the demos is exposed as far more illusory than might have been thought. While laid-off workers struggled to file for unemployment, small businesses shuttered, and entire industries teetered on the brink, financial markets still clawed for gains wherever possible, whipsawing daily but still reaping rewards for shrewd investors. It was never about the people; it was always about profits, accumulated by an elite few. So too the airline bailouts were less about restoring democratic access to flight than for keeping the whole economic pyramid intact—structurally holding up the very pinnacle, for as long as possible.

It is hard to believe that our current world will see an enthusiastic return to air travel. An email from Delta to its SkyMiles members pleaded for continued patience and understanding, underneath a seal that read, "Our Promise: Your Safety Above All." The problem, of course, is that Delta's promise was self-compromising: When people arrive everywhere safely, *so does the virus*. Our safety above all, at least for the foreseeable future, really means staying on the ground. Not flying.

We know that the novel coronavirus spread rapidly by plane, not just at the small scale of viral shedding potentially infecting those in a six-foot radius but also at the global scale of air travel, jumping across geopolitical borders. Commercial air travel is implicated and newly suspect, and it will likely remain so until there is proven vaccine for COVID-19, and/or herd immunity is acheived. Even if temperature scans become as common as X-ray machines and mandatory health certificates become as expected as passports, the sheer biology of epidemics will have undermined the untouchable symbolism of commercial flight. But it's more than symbolic: Flight is literally instrumental to the march of so-called progress.

I once wondered whether slick digital technologies such as phones in our pockets were compatible with the clunkiness of actual airplanes chugging up into the sky; it seemed like we were reaching a threshold where the speed and self-fulfilling premises of our personal devices would undermine the feasibility of the collective enterprise of queueing and sitting together to fly. But I never imagined the issue would be forced by something smaller than pixels—something in our body's cells. Zoom, Blue Jean, FaceTime, Google Hangouts, and Skype have now supplanted so many meetings that would have happened in person. And even if these media interfaces have already created their own forms of tedium and exhaustion, they've also become normalized with remarkable swiftness. It's almost as if the predictable speed of jet travel were transferred unconsciously over to these apps and windows. If business travelers and conference attendees had been conditioned to expect relatively seamless travel across thousands of miles, time zones, and cultural contexts, this same shared expectation made the mass transition to video conferencing so much easier over the past couple months.

The federal government's commitment to restoring commercial flight acts as if this pivot to virtual presence will be a temporary blip. But this attitude ignores the seismic shift that has taken place, articulated in the activism (epitomized now by Greta Thunberg) that has for years been flagging the environmental cost of excessive travel. It is likely that businesses that have become versant in Zoom and its ilk will cut travel budgets significantly rather than encourage their workers to Uber back to the airports in droves. Conferences and conventions, too, are transitioning to virtual formats.

The stimulus package offered bailout funds for the airlines so that workers could continue to be paid and aircraft could be kept ready to fly at a moment's notice—should the virus disappear, as in the "miracle" that Trump once touted. But the stimulus as written really just bought some time, a few months—while airline executives have pointed out that the economic damage is sure to be felt on a much longer timeline. As part of the stimulus arrangement, the Department of Transportation required that airlines receiving financial assistance "maintain minimum air services on a nationwide basis."[4] This recasts commercial flight as a kind of necessary evil, as a basic service, or even as a right—that *untouchable* aspect of aviation, itself now gasping for air. What if passenger demand never rebounds to even close to what it was prior to the pandemic, and for good reasons? But this question is anathema to leaders in government and the aviation industry alike.

Dreams of glamorous air travel have come back to Earth. The novel coronavirus may well be our Icarus moment. It's hard to imagine a return to sanguine treatments of flight after the curve has been flattened, when travelers, however tentatively, consider taking to the skies again. In six months, or a year, or two—if masses of people fly at all, depending on how things unfold—travelers may only want to get from point A to point B without catching COVID-19, not to mention instigating a *new* pandemic.

We'll want to know that airports are attuned to the potential of humans to be infectious, and not just trying to funnel us in and out as efficiently as possible. We'll be sensitized, perhaps, to the inconvenient facts of interconnectedness. Whereas once it was about *my* miles, *my* status, *my* legroom—social distancing practices have rejiggered our collective senses of space. And there's no way to simply soar above these new spatial constraints.

4. https://www.transportation.gov/sites/dot.gov/files/2020-03 /Order%202020-3-10%20FINAL.pdf.

Air travel is not over, not yet. But whatever comes next, we'll be more aware of how it is, inescapably, an organic planet that we live on—that we're always comingling with others, as well as with other species. Life on the ground will seem more heavy and less easily left behind.

Once upon a Time . . .

Remembering the Future of Flight

One thing I have done over the years is track how airports and air travel are depicted in popular culture. From TV shows and films to commercials and music, from magazine advertisements to contemporary art, such depictions can tell us a lot about what we expect from air travel in the present or how we imagine it in the future. And sometimes these fictive airports show what we may unconsciously fear we've *lost,* as flight has evolved over time.

So, for instance, you might recall that Brad Pitt starred in two big movies in 2019, the year before the pandemic: Quentin Tarantino's Oscar-winning retro film *Once Upon a Time . . . in Hollywood,* and James Grey's *Ad Astra,* a quiet and haunting film about a near-future space journey and a looming apocalypse. Besides having Brad Pitt as a main attraction, these films shared something else. Each one used airport scenes to set a mood and to communicate something. These brief scenes, in almost proleptic ways, can help us better understand the status of flight in the midst of the pandemic.

At one point late in *Once Upon a Time . . . in Hollywood,* the main characters are arriving home from a trip to Europe, and they are shown passing through the iconic mosaic-walled tunnel at LAX. First we see Leonardo DiCaprio's main character and his wife, played by Lorenza Izzo. And then we see Brad Pitt's supporting character bringing up the rear, pushing an absurdly piled-high cart of baggage for his boss. What was going on in this scene? On one level, it's just more vintage eye candy, thoroughly in line with the whole movie set in 1969, and in fact a favorite background of Tarantino's (he used the same hallway to begin his earlier film *Jackie Brown*). But there's something deeper—or more on the surface, rather—that I can't help but linger on. The airport hallway is all but empty: it accentuates the star status of the characters and makes every detail pop. In a way, this nearly empty airport scene was prescient of what was to come in early 2020.

When airports emptied almost overnight, and airliners were grounded everywhere, it seemed at first like a freak accident—how could the whole thing be so fragile, aborted so quickly? But the images captured around this time were striking, almost automatically cinematic—and, to me, they were reminiscent of what Tarantino was doing with LAX in *Once Upon a Time . . . in Hollywood*.

It felt like such an anomaly that some travelers recorded their experiences on social media, like one Instagram post by artist @ryn_wilson. The post read: "This is so surreal, like a post-apocalyptic film. I pretty much got my own airport today. Thanks Coronavirus."[1] The accompanying photographs showed a nearly empty gate area, and a nearly empty plane. A black-and-white filter neatly turned the scenes into something like historic photography. Like something from another time . . . but also, *our* time. The empty airport, once upon a time.

The ambivalence of this post is worth reflecting on. On the one hand, the everyday traveler recognized that flight had become

1. https://www.instagram.com/p/B9SgBGDFX16/?igshid= phm6qoca9zmj.

dysfunctional. It shouldn't have been this way—it was "post-apocalyptic." But on the other hand, the Instagrammer was pleasantly surprised by the empty gate area and plane, and reveling in it—even smug about the fact that they got their "own airport."

Empty airports. Is this what we really want, when it all comes down to it? Do we want to pass through empty (or nearly empty) airports, places there just for us exclusive travelers? Imagine the relative quiet, no lines, sit where you like—none of those annoying amateur fliers or self-absorbed million-milers. Just you and your own airport, facilitating your unique journey.

That's the wish image of airports, in some ways. I think about the empty terminal in New Orleans, before it opened. The as-yet-unused airport was stirring in all its polish and sleekness. It was also eerie—it felt wrong, somehow, to be wandering the concourses among no actual travelers. The airport opened with a few glitches, but general exuberance—it was a great new airport, and for the most part travelers loved the new restaurants, design features, and its general feel. We had no idea, then, that the airport would be nearly empty again so soon after its grand opening and a few months of record-breaking passenger counts.

These record-breaking numbers of travelers, of course, were also spreading the novel coronavirus for weeks, even months, before anyone realized it. Our new "world-class" airport was indeed performing as it promised it would: facilitating *global* travel, bringing tourists to town, showing off our city's cuisine and culture—but, also, it was accommodating the virus's own lines of flight. We wanted to see our new airport full of travelers coming and going; we didn't anticipate that all these travelers would indirectly cause the airport to become empty again, come late March.

The dilemma is a real one. Airports need to be busy in order to survive; airlines need passenger counts to be steady, if not always on the rise. Full planes and packed terminals mean revenue is being generated. Capitalism is growing growth. But a chaotic concourse can be harsh and vaguely depressing—air travel at full throttle can also feel like capitalism hates you. So airports look and feel better when they're emptier, but that's precisely not what they're made for. They're made to maximize people coming and going—until that very maximization causes a crisis that causes it all to come screeching to a halt.

I traveled through the Charlotte airport in late January 2020—the last time I flew. I was struck by how much of a mess this airport was. The floor was in tatters, the ceiling spewed utilities, signs were taped over, extension cords were draped here and there, and the acoustics were terrible. And still, everyone plodded toward their gates. Somehow we all understood that airports are giant works in progress, always. Some airports just show this a little more, in the midst of things. It can be slightly unnerving to show up for a flight with everything in total disarray right up to the point of the actual aircraft. If you've ever traveled through or into a terminal renovation in process, you know the feeling I'm talking about.

We're not done with Brad Pitt yet, though we are leaving him in the empty LAX of 1969, and finding him again around fifty years from now as an astronaut on a voyage to Neptune to retrieve his errant father, also an astronaut, played by Tommy Lee Jones. What caught my attention in Ad Astra were some early scenes that show a lunar base as, essentially, a grubby airport—not unlike the Charlotte airport as I experienced it in early 2020. There in the moon port we briefly see a DHL shipping store, a Subway, trudging passengers, garish if obscure corporate signage, and bored security personnel loitering about. The lunar base is rendered ordinary—just another cringe-worthy airport.

A few minutes earlier in the film, we see the departure back on Earth on a commercial rocket—the departure screen looking just like they do today, in LaGuardia or JFK or wherever: "GATE

4A . . . ON TIME . . . BOARDING at 16:00"—even a diagram of the rocket, so similar to how it might look when you see if you're flying an Airbus A320 or a Boeing 737. If you look very closely at this sign, you'll even notice that it's a branded trip: it's run by Virgin Atlantic. (It's hard to tell whether this appearance is intended as another branding shout-out or just an oversight in otherwise careful editing.)

When the passenger capsule arrives at the moon, its landing is completely normalized. Reaching out to the capsule is a familiar object: a jet bridge. I've been endlessly fascinated with these things, as they are the awkward in-between zones where you're neither in the airport, nor in the airplane.

These corridors are forgettable spaces, merely there to be passed through. (I can't imagine what social distancing has felt like in jet bridges—not easy or reassuring, I would guess.) We don't typically think of jet bridges as futuristic or as such an integral part of flight, which is why I always take note when they appear—whether in films *or* in other contexts.

When headlines were abuzz with news of that ultra-efficient Flying-V aircraft I wrote about earlier, I couldn't help but notice something in the concept illustrations: they had to show the plane hooked up to a jet bridge, as if to authenticate its proximity to actual reality. As if by adding that one design element, so common and trusted and overlooked, we could just imagine and wish our way to this new, greener plane.

And then there's Elon Musk. His successful May 2020 Crew Dragon launch, in partnership with NASA, utilized (and was staged and photographed from the vantage of) the astronauts' own jet bridge. Once again, what we see is an attempt to *normalize* what SpaceX also wanted to champion as a major achievement: sending American astronauts to space in an American vehicle, launched from American soil—a feat that hadn't been done since 2011. And it *was* a major achievement.

The lift-off was elegant and inspiring. (And the return, a few months later, no less so.)

But that jet bridge! It just made it seem so blasé. Interestingly, Musk himself has insisted time and again that the goal of SpaceX is precisely to make space travel as common and reliable *as* commercial air travel. For Musk, it is realistic and desirable to use the norms and expectations of commercial air travel to sell humans on far more risky, costly, and exclusive ventures: to the moon, and then to Mars, and then . . . beyond?

There's almost nothing so static in air travel over the past sixty-five years as the jet bridge. It's there, ready to board us onto the plane, and ready again to deplane us at our destinations. We learn how to move through these things unconsciously, lining up, inching forward, maneuvering our roller-bags . . . we rarely talk about them, but jet bridges are critical to the whole operation.

So in some ways, SpaceX's use of the perspective from the jet bridge is no surprise and is even tactical. And yet. I can't help but wonder how this recourse to the old form—the jet bridge— keeps things in a vicious cycle, rather than ushering in something revolutionary, something truly different. Commercial flight has been caught in this loop for some time—at least since Stanley Kubrick's 1968 film *2001: A Space Odyssey,* which depicted an orbiting space station with a relatively subdued waiting lounge. Even if jazzed up with bold color and high-modern design, it was still not so different from an everyday airport, with a hotel attached and plenty of seating for waiting passengers. The cushy red seats in that space station communicated everything: It all comes down to time to wait. (And if you can recall that scene, it *almost* looks like Kubrick anticipated social distancing, too!)

Similarly, the Pan-Am Space Clipper that transported the characters was another throwback—or forward—to our banal airliners. Sure, it's beyond Earth's atmosphere and headed to a space station, but it's basically like taking a transcontinental flight—window seats, cabin service, some time to recline your seat and doze. . . . Like in *Ad Astra*, it's as if science fiction can't quite cut its ties to these recurring themes and forms.

Commercial air travel has become caught in a sort of temporal bind. We know we need to move forward into the future, to change things for the better—and yet we seem stuck in certain ideas and shapes of the past. There is an old carpet in the Phoenix Sky Harbor airport that reminds me of this predicament: It depicts abstract airliners in interlinking and concentric—but perpetually closed—circles. We think we're taking flights ever forward, but we're really going around and around, bound to a past we can't seem to shake.

And there *are* a lot of things in the history of aviation worth marveling at, and celebrating. This is why many airports feature exhibits and displays that do justice to historic milestones in flight, such as Charles Lindbergh's planes hanging from the ceilings of St. Louis's Lambert airport. Or in the case of San Francisco International, the airport houses a brilliantly curated aviation museum and library. These examples celebrate the past of air travel, the triumphs and technological advances that we might indeed keep in mind as we ourselves pass through concourses and are lifted into the air.

Compare those two examples with a display I spotted in Washington Dulles in early 2019: "NASA and Dulles International are improving flight for you"—so reads a small mural positioned on the outside of a children's play area. It makes overtures to an alternative future of flight: there's a V-wing aircraft on the left, reminiscent of the Flying-V design and expected to make significant gains with respect to fuel efficiency. Then there's a diverse group of children in the center, holding kites, in a gesture toward renewable sources of energy—wind power, in this case. In the upper right, a fairly standard twin-engine airliner prepares to land. And all around, a verdant landscape reaches to the horizon.

While the poster is mostly whimsical, and light on persuasive complexity, it is nevertheless noteworthy for its focus on a future generation and (some) new modes of aviation. The language on the mural even states this directly: the airport is interested in the *improvement* of flight. Now this may just mean having a dedicated play area for children in the airport—which *is* a good idea!—but I can't help but detect grander ambitions at work.

But just what might such grander ambitions be, when the existing patterns that dictate air travel seem so set and established? The structures and routines of flight are fairly rigid and fixed, and for good reason: safety, predictability, consistency are of utmost importance.

How can human aviation advance technologically—even dramatically so—while aircraft manufacturers and airport infrastructure projects are dedicated to the continuation of flight essentially as is? In other words—and to stress a crucial point—aircraft manufacturers and airlines are designing, building, and using planes made to last thirty, forty, fifty years. Airport renovation and construction endeavors are likewise undertaken with several decades in mind. What impetus is there, really, for fundamental change?

Contemporary air travelers do not want to be surprised by new experiences in airports or to buy tickets to fly on experimental aircraft. For the past fifteen years or so, passengers and airlines did not expect air travel to change drastically. No one *wanted* such a drastic change, really.

And then came the novel coronavirus, and the pandemic that all but shut down commercial flight for several months. It was a shock to the system. Empty airports quickly stopped being novelties and became instead flashing economic warning signs. Planes were grounded in spectacular formations, showing in rare form the immense scale of this enterprise we call flight.

Niall Ferguson, in a *Wall Street Journal* opinion piece on March 8, called COVID-19's spread "a perfect illustration of the vulnerability and fragility of our networked world."[2] The illustration above this piece was oddly playful: bulbous little airliners zipping around the sky, with a cartoonish, human-face-sized coronavirus sitting in a window seat of one plane, flying along with normal human passengers.

Ferguson's observations in this piece were largely correct, but throughout the spring there was a sort of cultural schizophrenia about the role that air travel played in relation to the pandemic. Airline executives urged travelers to stay safe but keep flying. President Trump limited air travel from certain places, thereby acknowledging the gravity of the situation, but as air travel continued at a frantic pace throughout the country (not to mention much of the world) through the early spring, the pandemic was exacerbated. Airplanes and airports were undoubtedly significant superspreaders. Still, we kept flying.

New aircraft cleaning procedures were put in place, if inconsistently. "Fogging" became almost a meme, as if to reassure travelers that planes could be so thoroughly disinfected between flights. (Having cleaned planes between flights myself, I can assure you that it's almost always a harried exercise in futility.)

Passengers who had always obsessively wiped down their seatback tray tables and armrests proved to be ahead of the times; now everyone was doing it. (Or, all six people on a 150-passenger plane, anyway.) Empty planes are better for social distancing, but economically not very viable for airlines—not for long anyway. And some planes during the pandemic were ending up chock-full of passengers, with no firm guidelines in terms of social distanc-

2. https://www.wsj.com/articles/network-effects-multiply-a-viral
-threat-11583684394.

ing or mask wearing—making a mockery of the very protocols that all but certainly saved millions of lives.

Meanwhile, entrepreneurial visionaries propose cheery alternative configurations for aircraft seating so as to reduce the risk of viral spread—like one concept for a new seating arrangement, by AvioInteriors. The idea was that by sitting in staggered formation, face to face, with curving transparent plastic walls between each passenger, the problem could be solved. But as some early critics pointed out, it might be a little too awkward to be basically staring at your seatmate's face a few inches away, for an entire flight. An early design brief showed one masked passenger, and another unmasked—the unmasked traveler smiling happily. This image belied something more troubling about how democratic commercial flight promises to welcome and accept a range of travelers and their varying individual values and beliefs; but when it comes to a virus, there are limits to how such values and beliefs can (or *can't*) coexist in such close proximity.

It may be tempting to think that this will all blow over, that soon the masks and face shields and constant hand sanitizing will become relics of the past. Commercial air travel has felt like such a constant, for so long, for so many of us. Even if we only fly once a year or less, we would know basically what to expect. Is it really possible that the entire system has been so disrupted—and will remain disrupted for a long time, even to the point of having to change in ways we can't yet imagine?

If you are convinced that this is only a temporary blip, and that we'll be back in the friendly skies in a matter of months or a year, consider that nearly twenty years after September 11, 2001, we're still trudging through an entirely changed security screening process, procedures and rules that were adopted in response to the terrorist attacks of that day and several threats in the months after. Most of us still take off our shoes to pass through security (talk about unhygienic), after one failed attempt at shoe-bombing a plane in December 2001. Many of us still travel with miniscule bottles of shampoo and conditioner and toothpaste, after rumors and reports concerning possible liquid bombs. We submit to having our bodies sprayed with small doses of radiation, hands in the air.

The atrocities of the 9/11 attacks were of course serious, but we should ask what a proportionate response may be in 2021 and beyond, after hundreds of thousands of COVID-related deaths and newly awakened awareness—if not outright fear—of the likelihood of a *next* pandemic.

The truth is, air travel occupies an exceptional place in the world—and especially in the most developed parts of the world. Almost no other place is protected like an airport. Not shopping malls, not Costcos or Home Depots, not school buildings or college campuses, not bustling office parks, not churches or synagogues or temples, not concert halls or museums . . . not even movie theaters. Airports are privileged zones of exception, and they are guarded as such. The reason is a combination of air travel being such a functional part of global capitalism, as well as flight being symbolic of human progress on a more transcendental level.

So when it comes to thinking about the long-range effects of the pandemic on air travel, we have to keep in mind how uniquely vulnerable flight is—and how *implicated* airplanes become in a viral spread.

It's worth noting how the coronavirus has been described as 'hijacking' human cells. This is how an infographic that accompanied a *New York Times* article in March put it: "How coronavirus hijacks your cells."[3] That metaphor is of course borrowed from air travel and terrorism: *airplanes* are hijacked. If that's how

3. https://www.nytimes.com/interactive/2020/03/11/science/how -coronavirus-hijacks-your-cells.html.

we understand the virus, you can be sure the domain of flight itself will take this threat seriously as such.

In early June 2020, American Airlines sent out a news release announcing "A New Look for New York: American Airlines Welcomes Customers to a Reimagined Arrivals and Departures Hall at LaGuardia Airport."[4] It was an odd document, part a celebration of a new terminal at a widely reviled airport, and part an acknowledgment of the radically changed landscape with fewer people flying, and those who are flying more conscious than ever of personal risk and public health. The announcement featured three photographs of the new terminal, and they were revealing.

The first photograph showed off the new departures area, with check-in kiosks spaced out responsibly and hand-wipe stations prominent. Intriguingly—and an all-too-familiar theme, by now—the space was empty. No airline workers ready to serve, no travelers in action. It was another empty airport, directly through the first sliding doors.

The second photograph was of the baggage claim, with an "I ♥ NY" sign and a piece of "custom artwork" hanging from the ceiling. Again, not a soul could be seen in this sparkling space. I want to bring us back to my earlier question: Do we *want* airports to be empty? Are they best seen and experienced this way? Or does such imagery cast airports wrongly as an impossibly rarified experience—and as such, as an unsustainable enterprise?

The third photograph returned to the arrivals and departures hall—and we finally were presented with a human. A human

4. https://news.aa.com/news/news-details/2020/A-New-Look-for -New-York-American-Airlines-Welcomes-Customers-to-a-Reimagined -Arrivals-and-Departures-Hall-at-LaGuardia-Airport-OPS-INF-06 /default.aspx.

wearing a *mask*. The pandemic strikes back. This image also featured another view of the suspended artwork, from straight on—a form that uncannily resembles a coronavirus! At least I couldn't help but see a vague resemblance to this now so commonly represented shape. Am I stretching things a bit, has my imagination got the better of me? Maybe. But we've been inundated by apparitions of this spherical, spiky form.

I feel like I saw one particular image ten times a day throughout the spring—it was the go-to coronavirus image, red and grey on a dark background. CNN even used it to advertise a coronavirus "fact vs. fiction" podcast . . . right beneath an ad featuring none other than—Brad Pitt! Perpetual flight always comes full circle.

Back in LaGuardia, American Airlines attempts to adjust to this new normal, tries to win back customers, and tries to help us make sense of the future to come.

But if we're honest with ourselves, we don't really know, yet, what this will entail. Will the virus be vanquished and air travel restored to its full splendor? I don't think it will be that easy or that clear. Especially now that the realities of living in a viral, networked world have been made so plain, and so real, for so many.

Will as many people want to travel, if it means getting temperature scanned when passing through, and perhaps having to show health papers? If it means not knowing if you're going to have a plane to yourself, or be scrunched in next to a possibly contagious seatmate? If it means having to wear a mask, or at least having to have one on hand, in case? If it means having your flight suddenly rerouted if a fellow passenger falls ill midair?

And in the meantime, for how long will airlines be able to hobble along with planes that are nearly empty? Will airlines begin to consolidate or merge, and what will happen to air fares

and amenities as these shifts take place? Airlines won't show
their cards to the public until things get really bad—we don't
know yet which airlines are tipping on the edge of solvency and
which might no longer exist in a few months, or a year. I remember watching vibrant red Northwest planes fly in and out of
Bozeman—now just a memory. Northwest was absorbed by Delta
in 2008, many of their jets lying in airplane graveyards. These
things happen fast, and then we tend to forget about them. We're
likely on the verge of major changes with regard to airlines as
we know them today.

Could this moment usher in new interest and investment
in high-speed rail, particularly in the United States, as a more
grounded alternative to air travel? Will people recommit to more
local, closer adventures? What are other potential upsides of a
collective, newfound wariness of flight?

As I was finishing this book, CNN featured an article that
asked whether it was safer to fly or drive during the pandemic.
The lead image that accompanied the piece, of masked passengers in an airliner with empty middle seats, seemed to nudge
readers toward flight. The article was basically a prosaic shrug:
It all depends. Weigh the pros and cons, figure out which is going to involve more exposure, and decide what makes the most
sense for *you*.

But remember our superorganism status: Every single individual decision, taken collectively, affects the whole. Each passenger
who chooses to fly amplifies the effects of flight. This was always
true; now it's just been made more obvious and public, with the
realities of a disease that we still are learning about and for which
we have no vaccine.

You might choose to fly during this time, and statistically
speaking, *you* will probably be fine. But it's not just a personal
risk. Every person who flies in the coming months and years contributes to the exponential potential of viral spread: airports and

airplanes are unavoidably "high touch" zones, where viruses can thrive—fogging and hand sanitizing stations notwithstanding. As more people take to the air again, the risks ripple outward, around the planet. Right now, we can grasp this as a public health matter. But there are other economic and environmental ripple effects, as well, that we will have to contend with in the coming years. A pandemic is just one of several imminent calamities in store, if we keep going this way.

What would it mean for people to deliberately choose to fly less often? How could this change business practices, tourism, and family trips—possibly in ways we might benefit from? Could commercial flight be reconceived as an enterprise with 90 percent less demand and supply, and end up better for it? I think these are real questions worth asking ourselves.

Whatever happens, air travel has probably changed definitively. And it will probably keep changing into the next several years—in ways we can't yet imagine. The downside of this is that we can't expect it all to return to "normal," whatever that felt like for the past several decades.

The upshot, though, is that we can be a part of this time of great change, and we can help shape what this change looks like and means for our species—and for our world.

Acknowledgments

Thank you to Lara for putting up with me while I wrote one more book about airports. Thanks to Doug Armato, Harriet Baskas, Tom Beller, Patrick Bixby, Ian Bogost, Torie Bosch, Whitney Dangerfield, Dana Gainey, and Rob Horning for editorial feedback, suggestions, and support as I worked on this project. Thanks to the team at University of Minnesota Press for making a home for this little book in the intrepid Forerunners series.

(Continued from page iii)

Forerunners: Ideas First

Sohail Daulatzai
Fifty Years of *The Battle of Algiers*: Past as Prologue

Gary Hall
The Uberfication of the University

Mark Jarzombek
Digital Stockholm Syndrome in the Post-Ontological Age

N. Adriana Knouf
How Noise Matters to Finance

Andrew Culp
Dark Deleuze

Akira Mizuta Lippit
Cinema without Reflection: Jacques Derrida's Echopoiesis and Narcissism Adrift

Sharon Sliwinski
Mandela's Dark Years: A Political Theory of Dreaming

Grant Farred
Martin Heidegger Saved My Life

Ian Bogost
The Geek's Chihuahua: Living with Apple

Shannon Mattern
Deep Mapping the Media City

Steven Shaviro
No Speed Limit: Three Essays on Accelerationism

Jussi Parikka
The Anthrobscene

Reinhold Martin
Mediators: Aesthetics, Politics, and the City

John Hartigan Jr.
Aesop's Anthropology: A Multispecies Approach

Christopher Schaberg is Dorothy Harrell Brown Distinguished Professor of English at Loyola University New Orleans and author of five books, including most recently *The Work of Literature in an Age of Post-Truth* and *Searching for the Anthropocene: A Journey into the Environmental Humanities.*